Strategy Implementation: Readings

PJ Smit (Compiler)

PN Palmer

MA van der Merwe

First Published 2000

© Juta & Co Ltd 2000

PO Box 14373,
Kenwyn
7790

ISBN 0 7021 5547 0

Editors: Pearson Editorial cc
Book design and typesetting: Lebone Publishing Services
Cover design: Dallas du Toit
Printed and bound in South Africa by: Creda Communications,
Eliot Avenue, Eppindust II, Cape Town.

Contents

Preface

'The best game plan in the world never blocked or tackled anybody' (Lombardi in David, *Strategic Management Concepts* 1999:215).

To be considered effective, a chosen strategy must be implemented successfully. The ability to translate the strategic plan into actions and generate positive outcomes can itself be a source of competitive advantage.

However, this translation of thoughts (strategic planning) into action (strategy implementation and control) causes a major challenge. The profound differences between strategic planning, and strategy implementation and control, are exacerbated by the fact that different groups of managers are involved in the two processes. This holds the danger of the plans 'getting lost' in the strategic management process.

The implementation and control of the chosen strategy or strategies require the strategic manager to consider, among others, the following catalysts:

- the structure to support the chosen strategy or strategies
- appropriate leadership
- meaningful resource allocation
- a complementary organisational culture
- appropriate reward systems
- a strategic control system

This compilation of articles deals with the above issues. The articles are grouped into four sections:

1. Strategy implementation: an overview
2. Strategy implementation and leadership
3. Translating strategic thought into action
4. Strategic control

The point of departure in selecting the relevant articles for this compilation was that learners need to master certain specific outcomes. To do this they have to master the relevant knowledge, skills and attitudes pertaining to strategy implementation and control and be able to apply these in different contexts. A textbook alone cannot achieve this.

This particular compilation allows *Strategy implementation: readings* to be used either in conjunction with other study material or as a stand-alone prescribed book. This book is a follow-up to *Strategic planning: readings,* which comprises articles dealing with this phase of the strategic management process.

Copyright permission has been obtained to use the original articles in the book. Consequently there is no consistency in referencing styles or language and grammar usage. We are governed by the styles used in each of the individual articles.

Should you come across articles or excerpts that you consider merit placement in the next edition, you are welcome to contact me:

cell 082 44 25707

e-mail pjsmit@iafrica.com

Your contribution will be much appreciated, and I trust that you will enjoy this compilation of readings.

Professor Pieter J Smit
University of South Africa

Strategy Implementation: an Overview

A Pragmatic Approach to Vision

Bob Frisch

Bob Frisch, vice president of Gemini Consulting, has led numerous visioning projects and helped develop Vision Engineering, Gemini's vision development process.

Source: *Journal of Business Strategy,* July/August 1998, pp. 12-15.

The vision thing. George Bush downplayed it; Lou Gerstner said it was the last thing IBM needed, and it makes many executives uncomfortable. It's easy to see why. On the one hand, vision often means stirring slogans and ambitious generalities, but too few details about how to realize them. On the other, it sometimes means betting the company on some highly speculative view of the future.

Meanwhile, what many senior executives really want to know is where the next growth opportunities are going to come from, how to pursue them, and how to align their management team around them.

Those senior executives have the right instincts. Vision should be concrete, not abstract. It should be based on facts, not speculation. Equally important, if the vision is to produce results, it must be widely understood and enthusiastically embraced throughout the organization.

Such workable, winning visions don't just happen. They crucially depend on the vision development process itself. A poor process will produce poor results – "garbage in, garbage out," as the systems people say. Having no process – such as treating strategy development as part of the budget and planning function – makes vision an afterthought. Yet the wilder forms of visioning – conjuring up images of navel-gazing or free-form brainstorming sessions – can be as alienating as having no process at all.

A successful visioning process requires the application of some very practical principles – principles that keep your feet firmly planted on the ground. Despite that practicality, however, they run contrary to much of what we ordinarily think about vision, creativity, and the best way to pursue new opportunities. Nevertheless, there are 10 principles that should be the starting point for answering the hard questions about where you should take your company.

Effective vision development is a straightforward activity. It's not magic bullets or blinding revelations – and there are no shortcuts.

You're heading to a three-day off-site to hammer out your company's vision for the future. Expectations are high. You hope that the hothouse atmosphere of the meetings will generate blinding revelations about the future direction of the company. After all, that's what vision means: seeing the big picture all at once, in a dazzling flash of insight. But is that a realistic expectation? Perhaps for entrepreneurs working on a start-up company in a garage. But is it likely that a huge, complex, modern business enterprise will secure success on the strength of sudden revelation? That would be a miracle indeed.

Effective vision development is a far more pedestrian activity. It's less about revelation than conversation. It means a group of executives reaching a mutual understanding about opportunities, capabilities, and assets. It is a conversation that must be structured, logical, and carried on over time, interwoven with a great deal of preparation and analytical work.

At the end of this conversation, a vision should emerge that is widely understood and widely shared and that is therefore far more likely to be implemented effectively. Such a no-nonsense process may or may not produce blinding insights, but it will certainly produce blinding results.

In successfully pursuing vision, leadership alignment is as important as creativity.

Creativity certainly counts, but the most creative vision means nothing if it cannot be put into action. When members of the leadership team do not share a common understanding of the forces shaping their world, the result is likely to be a vision that is poorly understood, easily misinterpreted, and difficult to implement in a coordinated fashion. Nevertheless, surveys Gemini Consulting has conducted in many companies reveal weak alignment around the major forces driving the enterprise's vision. In fact, in many cases, it is alignment, rather than new opportunities, that many companies most sorely need. Vision development that does not create leadership alignment tends to produce the proverbial vision that "looks good on paper" but falters in practice.

You cannot outsource vision.

It's no secret that the field of vision and corporate strategy is heavily populated with gurus, futurists, and consultants. It is tempting to call in these outside experts for a presumably objective view of the opportunities your company should pursue.

Unfortunately, even if external experts do supply a plausible vision, there are two crucial things they cannot provide. First, they cannot supply the leadership alignment that is a prerequisite for successful implementation. Second, they do not leave your team with the skill to do its own strategy work in the future.

It is extremely difficult to gain leadership alignment at the conclusion of an outside vendor's vision development process. The only way to ensure early and thorough alignment around a vision is through direct participation in its formulation. Your leadership team should be involved in the creation of the vision from the first step to the last, agreeing on its assumptions and understanding its implications for every aspect of the business.

Building strategy is a team skill. Many companies today are more than willing to have their managers spend a week rafting down a river together to build a better team. And it works.

Managers come back communicating better – and very good at rafting down rivers. But how many businesses devote the same time and intensity to forging a team that is good at building strategies together?

In the course of building a strategy, the team acquires the ability to think as a group about strategic issues. They develop not only a strategy, but also a permanent strategy-development capability. If you outsource the development process to consultants, your team members won't acquire those skills, and your organization will be left without an invaluable capability. Where consultants can be helpful is in creating a process for your team to use and in populating that process with information.

Making executives uncomfortable during vision exercises does not produce "stretch" visions; it merely produces uncomfortable executives.

Executives who are quite comfortable within their areas of expertise may feel exposed if they are expected to suddenly provide brilliant visions. After all, they are not part of the strategy team because they are visionaries; they are there because they represent key parts of the organization.

In fact, although we call such groups executive teams, they much more closely resemble legislative bodies. There is a representative from operations, a representative from finance, a representative from marketing, and so on. Vision did not bring these "representatives" to the pinnacle of their functional areas, competence in their specialties did. But now they are cast in a role unlike any they've had before. Not surprisingly, they feel uncomfortable.

Unfortunately, many methods of vision development either ignore the issue altogether or assume that discomfort will produce "stretch" visions by forcing executives into unfamiliar territory. Such approaches alienate executives rather than bring them together as a team. It is far better to manage the process so that it looks and feels like the other things executives do. It should differ little from the business-like, structured environments with which executives are familiar and in which they have always thrived. It should bring the team along together in its understanding. Above all, it should re-create the conditions that have allowed them to succeed in the past. "Sink or swim" may or may not be a good approach in some endeavors, but it certainly does not work in vision development.

The more structured the vision planning process is, the more creativity it will yield.

Contrary to prevailing clichés about creativity, structure doesn't inhibit originality; it enables it. Shakespeare wrote sonnets, one of the most rigid and demanding forms imaginable, requiring 14 lines of strict poetic meter and adherence to an unvarying rhyme scheme. Far from inhibiting him, this familiar structure unleashed his creativity, spurring him to write some of the most original and enduring work in any language. Similarly, in team sports, the creativity of the athlete blossoms only within a defined set of rules.

Not surprisingly, what works in other fields of human creativity applies as well to business. A highly structured approach to vision development yields more, not less, creativity. Each step in the process, supported by compelling research and analysis, should flow logically from the preceding one. Executives know exactly what to expect and what is expected of them in the process.

What is not known beforehand is the outcome – the content of the vision. That is where true creativity comes in, arising out of the structure and preparation that allow the most productive possible use of executives' time. As the team builds momentum, the structure channels their creativity into the most productive paths. Like the artist or the athlete, the executive flourishes because of the structure, not in spite of it.

The starting point for formulating your strategy is not your company – or your competitors.

Where do you start to build a vision? Far too many companies begin by looking internally, while keeping one eye on the competition. But neither your internal capabilities nor your competitors' actions are the ultimate arbiter of your fate. The world is.

Economic, social, technological, and other powerful forces occurring in the world will determine the shape of your industry and the future of your business. Those are the forces that should drive your vision, and they do not originate inside your company. Moreover, they dwarf any single corporation. Some years ago, Bill Gates famously warned his colleagues at Microsoft – a seemingly invulnerable company with a lock on the future – that the firm must confront the coming Internet "tidal wave." It's an apt comparison. The forces in the outside world are like enormous waves threatening to engulf your industry and your company. It is at those oncoming waves that you should look first, not at your particular boat bobbing in the water.

There is another, equally compelling reason for looking outside the walls first. One of the most difficult things for a functional manager to do is to step outside that functional role and think about the company as a whole. If the discussion begins with the company itself, it becomes even more difficult. Again, like the members of a legislative body, functional managers will naturally and aggressively represent the interests of their constituencies. By considering external forces first, you induce functional managers to look at the issues from the perspective of a general manager. As they begin to reach a shared understanding of those external forces and a consensus about how they will affect the company, the likelihood decreases that they will fall back into narrowly functional views when the focus turns inward.

Documented trends provide a sounder basis for vision than uncertainties.

Conventional wisdom assumes that the greatest opportunities lie along the path of uncertainty, where bold corporate gamblers base their visions on highly conjectural views of the future. But there are a great many opportunities that do not involve speculative wagers on the future.

For example, for CNN the opportunity to create a 24-hour cable news network did not spring from "betting" about the future appetite of viewers for more news. Instead, it was based on the confluence of well-documented social, technological, and business trends that were already underway:

- Lengthening and unpredictability of working hours
- Decrease in cost and increase in portability of video technology
- Deregulation of cable television
- Proliferation of independent television stations
- Habituation of consumers to television programming on demand

Establishing CNN did, of course, entail risks, but those risks lay in the implementation of the concept, not in whether new competitive space was emerging in the industry.

By seeing how well-documented trends open up new competitive space, companies can build long-term sustainable advantage while controlling downside risks. Although uncertainty can sometimes create powerful opportunities, so can already identified trends – and with a far higher likelihood of success.

Unfortunately, many vision development methods ask you to imagine several possible futures and then place a bet on which one is most likely to come to pass. Although powerful analytical tools like scenario planning were never intended to be used in this way, in actual practice they often encourage a "casino" approach to strategy formulation. But by basing your team's mutual understanding of the future on well-documented trends, you can systematically eliminate the risk inherent in such approaches.

There is great benefit to be derived from the obvious.

Knowledge of particular external trends is available to many people. But that is simply another way of saying those trends are reliable and well-established, guaranteeing that your ultimate vision rests on a factual basis. Equally important, as your team reaches agreement about the validity of those trends, the process of alignment begins. In addition, once you can agree about where and how the waves will hit, you can map your present initiatives against them.

The obvious may also lead to the not-so-obvious. As you begin to see how related groups of trends are forming powerful waves of the future, your team may produce frame-breaking insights. One of the most effective ways to identify such opportunities is through a process we call "slamming" – forcefully superimposing oncoming trends on the existing value chain and product/market combinations.

The resulting collision throws into dramatic relief the disruptions and distortions that are likely to occur – and the opportunities that will emerge. What new competitive space will open up in your value chain? What new market and product opportunities will appear? It's not the much-vaunted "out-of-the-box" thinking, but something far more crucial to your company's future: how that box is likely to change.

Uncertainty has its place in vision development, and that place is at the end of the process.

Although it is unwise to base your vision development process on uncertainties, you must eventually take them into account.

For example, uncertainties can be used to generate scenarios with which to test the robustness of possible visions. This process resembles scenario planning, but with a crucial difference. Scenario planning, as it is often executed, asks you to choose just one of several uncertainty-based scenarios. Instead, consider creating risk profiles and business cases for several possible visions, each of which is based on documented trends. You introduce risk only at the end of the process and put it in its proper place – as a final testing mechanism for the vision, not as its foundation.

The vision should be developed in a way that optimizes its implementation.

The way in which a vision is developed directly determines the likelihood of its successful implementation. The principles laid out here produce precisely that kind of synergy:

- Early and thorough alignment around the forces shaping your world produces the coordinated effort necessary for thorough implementation once the vision emerges.
- A structured approach to vision development builds momentum and points the way forward.
- The vision's basis in certainty promotes organization-wide buy-in, leading to faster mobilization and implementation.

Meanwhile, the clear audit trail that runs back to the factual foundation of the vision offers a guide for the design of operational specifics. Most important of all, the strategy-building skills your team acquires provide a permanent capacity to monitor the progress of implementation against the vision and to quickly make adjustments as conditions change.

Whether the goal of your vision development is to uncover new opportunities, to produce alignment, or to do both, these principles offer the best chance of success. What they may lack in futurist flashiness, they more than make up in the reliability, clarity, and effectiveness that they bring to your vision development. Your vision works in the real world because it is grounded, not grandiose. It is produced through structure, not serendipity. And it is widely shared as a result of participation, not pronouncements.

You create vision in order to create value. Good vision development shortens the distance between the two.

Is Strategy Making a Difference?

J. Moncrieff

James Moncrieff is a Client and Programme Director at Ashridge Strategic Management Centre, London, UK and consults to Boards and groups of senior managers on strategy process.

Source: *Long Range Planning,* Vol. 32, No. 2, 1999, pp. 273-276.

If you want a thought-provoking insight into strategy, try an apparently simple test. First, take your company's most recent Annual Report and examine the descriptions of where your organization is now and where it is going. Then track back through previous years to find where today's position is articulated in some form of strategy. So ... how did your organization get to where it is today?

McGill's Henry Mintzberg[1] points out that not all *intended strategies* are realized, and not all *realized strategies* were intended. Realized strategy is often *emergent* in nature. While Mintzberg's view of strategy usually strikes a chord with managers, they often struggle with his different 'strategies'. However, they usually identify three sources of strategic outcome:

- Implementation of earlier strategic intent.
- Deliberate responses to issues emerging within the competitive environment.
- The results of the actions of people, working in ignorance of the strategy or of how they contribute to its implementation.

The first covers Mintzberg's *intended and deliberate strategies.* The second can still usefully be labelled *emergent strategy,* as it is based on responses to *emerging* opportunities and threats. They are the result of deliberate decisions to marshal and focus resources in order to pursue a new direction, modifying or replacing some aspects of earlier strategic intent, a process which Mintzberg refers to as *strategic learning.*

The third, however, might best be labelled *strategy in action,* as it is the result of the actions of many people throughout the organization, rather than the intentions of a few at the top. It modifies the outcomes of earlier strategic intent, without the "knowing, deliberate decisions" described above. It rarely becomes formalized as strategy and so, rarely results in strategic learning.

These labels, and what lies behind them provide the building blocks of a new model of strategy as a dynamic process. This process involves ... the formation of strategic intent, the alignment of action with intent, and the response to emerging issues, as well as the learning which is deeply implicated in all three (Fig. 1).

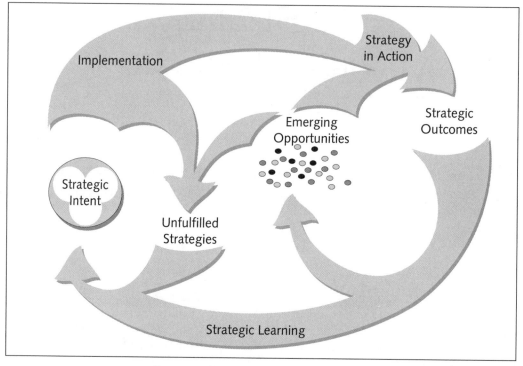

Figure 1. Strategy: a dynamic process.

We can use this model for discussing three common strategic questions:

- How should strategic intent be formed?
- How to align action with intent?
- How to become responsive to emerging issues?

Strategy Formation

Different strategic schools tend to emphasis either analysis or visioning as the source of strategic intent. However, two other factors can have at least as much influence. Firstly, people do not enter the process as empty vessels. They bring their prior learning, assumptions and beliefs. Secondly, strategy formation usually involves a group of people, with real issues at stake, so it can be subject to the influence of both the social dynamics of the group and the political dynamics of the organization. Strategy formation, therefore, involves four elements: analysis, visioning, assumptions and sociopolitical dynamics (Fig. 2).

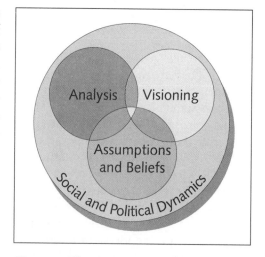

Figure 2. Elements in strategy formation.

Cranfield's Gerry Johnson suggests that strategic decisions are best explained in terms of political processes rather than analytical procedures.[2] He contends that the mental maps of managers influence their perception more than formal analysis, and these mental maps are reinforced through the culture of the organization to become what we refer to as *paradigms.* Paradigms can become so deeply ingrained that they are invisible and unquestioned 'truths'. Johnson suggests that both intended and realized strategies are likely to be configured within the parameters of the paradigm: " ... we need to distinguish between the paradigm and the strategy".

The trouble is that deeply held paradigms have significant implications for the formation of strategy, particularly if the changes needed are substantial. Paradigms dull organizational senses. Hamel[3] talks about "listening to new voices" but ... with strong paradigms who will listen?

Harvard's Chris Argyris[4] describes learning in terms of a double loop process, which involves uncovering and challenging the assumptions and beliefs that have been formed and reinforced through prior learning.

Managers, Argyris argues, are likely to listen to new voices and hear their message only if they are open to uncovering and challenging their own assumptions and beliefs. Strategy formation thus becomes a learning process for managers and the organization. Managers must recognize and then challenge their own assumptions and beliefs, and those paradigms held collectively by the organization.

Analysis can provide managers with objective data which may challenge those beliefs, while the creative tension between the data and the beliefs can stimulate fresh and innovative thinking. These new 'visions' can in turn be subjected to analysis for a reality check (Fig. 3).

Finally, analysis can provide objective data to combat any political forces that may influence the process and the outcomes. These forces often exist when new strategies require restructuring at a senior level or when they threaten to undermine existing power bases. Analysis, therefore is at the core of strategy formation, but it is by no means the whole story.

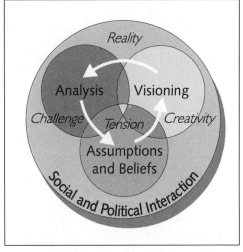

Figure 3. Forming innovative strategies.

The key is to develop analytical processes and follow-up dialogues which do not collude with and reinforce the paradigm, but encourage and enable it to be questioned and challenged. An outside agent can bring added value and rigour to the process: by resisting pressure to collude, by holding the tension when challenging the paradigm, and by surfacing and facilitating the resolution of political undertones. A role is very different from the typical data gathering and number crunching of strategy consultants.

Successful strategy formation, therefore, involves carefully balancing and blending the four elements of analysis, visioning, assumptions and socio-political dynamics.

Aligning Action with Intent

It is one thing to communicate a clear understanding of the vision and strategy, but quite another to align with the strategy the diverse forces that drive the actions of employees. Four such forces stand out as having great influence on the decisions and actions of people. These forces can be so powerful that they can drive behaviour that is actually contrary to the declared strategy:

1. What people think they are rewarded for

This is not necessarily as simple as it sounds. A database company sought growth through high margin value added products and services, such as consultancy, training, support and maintenance. But, the sales force were rewarded for monthly database licence sales. They quickly discovered that to sell 'commodity' database licences in a saturated market with a relatively fixed price book they had to give away additional services, such as consultancy, training, support and maintenance.

2. What people think they are measured on

A food manufacturing company had a long tail of low margin commodity products that needed to be rationalized. But, two key measures, overhead recovery and capacity utilization drove Operations to push anything through the machines so long as it kept them running and spread the overhead costs, regardless of the impact on the rest of the business.

3. What the boss appears to see as important

A financial services system provider had several strategic priorities. But, the divisional director was interested in growth not delivery. His constant challenging on growth targets led managers to win undeliverable business, so the growth was unsustainable.

4. What they did yesterday

Days of repetition can become months, even years. What a sobering thought ... that the strategic outcomes of many organizations may be the result of the efforts of people simply doing what they did yesterday – a kind of institutional inertia.

Many techniques have promised, in one way or another, to align action with intent, from MBO to MBWA. Yet, just a few simple steps can have quite an impact:

- Firstly, to help people recognize the relevance of their contribution to the overriding objectives of the organization.
- Secondly, to agree clear objectives – expectations of people in terms of priorities and performance.
- Thirdly, to link measures and rewards to those things that are important for strategic change, as well as those important to operational performance.
- Fourthly, to provide regular review with consistent, focused rigour.

It should be remembered that simply aligning action with intent can be dangerous. The company's competitive advantage may be the result of *action:* responding to customer, supplier, delivery, quality problems; rather than *intent:* such as to be a world class service company. Aligning action with intent may serve to reduce success rather than increase it. It may be better at times to consider aligning intent with action – aligning strategy with the core competencies of the organization.

Response to Emerging Issues

The process of response to emerging issues is not dissimilar to the psychological response to external stimuli: sensing, awareness, motivation to act, movement or action. Sensing and awareness are often seen in organizations as data gathering and analysis, but this is only part of the process. Sensing begins at the boundaries and is the role of everyone, whether they are interfacing with customers, suppliers, regulators or market analysts, etc. However, they have to believe that it is part of their role and that they will be listened to.

Strategic awareness is much more than simply analysing the data. It requires the ability to differentiate between operational and strategic emerging issues. Strategic awareness requires both insight and foresight, *and* it requires the courage to move to the next stage which may mean challenging the current strategy.

The ability to respond to emerging strategic issues requires more than just flexibility within the organization. Richard Pascale uses the term *agility* to describe "the sustainable capacity for change".[5] Agility carries connotations of both poise and balance as well as flexibility and responsiveness. It suggests that emergent strategy requires considered managed change which is equally mindful of the need for continuity. Above all, organizational agility requires managers never to think they have finally "got it right".

The Essence of Strategy?

- **Strategy appears to be a learning process:** a double loop learning process which seeks to challenge assumptions and beliefs, to shift paradigms and create visions of the future.

- **Strategy appears to be an action process:** a dynamic, directed yet responsive, action process with poise and balance.

- **Strategy appears to be a behavioural process:** a set of non-political behaviours – listening, challenging and being open to challenge.

- **Strategy appears to be a holistic, continuous process:** which we disintegrate through theories, models, frameworks and labels, in order to understand and talk about; but which we have trouble re-integrating as an interactive and interdependent whole.

References

1. H. Mintzberg, Patterns in strategy formation, *Management Science* May (1978).
2. G. Johnson, Rethinking incrementalism, in D. Asch and C. Bowman (eds), *Readings in Strategic Management,* Macmillan, London (1989).
3. G. Hamel and C.K. Prahalad, Competing for the future, *Harvard Business Review* July-August (1994).
4. C.A. Argyris, R. Putnam and D. McLainSmith, *Action Science,* Jossey Bass, New York (1985).
5. R. Pascale, M. Millemann and L. Gioja, Dinosaurs to butterflies, Draft (1996).

The Eclectic Roots of Strategy Implementation Research

Charles H. Noble

Charles H. Noble is attached to the Marketing Department, The Wallace E. Carroll School of Management, Boston College, Chestnut Hill, MA 02467-3808.

Source: *Journal of Business Research* 45, (1999) 119-134.

The researcher interested in strategy implementation faces a formidable challenge. Although this area has drawn many calls for research attention, there is not a deep and cohesive body of prior literature on which to draw in developing new efforts. This study proposes that through taking a broadened perspective of the nature of implementation, a range of valuable insights for the implementation researcher is available. First, various conceptualizations and definitions of implementation that have been proposed are considered. Next, a broad range of literature fields that have direct and indirect implications for the study of strategy implementation are reviewed. This review is organized around a framework that distinguishes between structural and interpersonal process views of implementation. Insights for the implementation researcher are highlighted. Finally, future directions for implementation research are proposed.

Well-formulated strategies only produce superior performance for the firm when they are successfully implemented (cf. Bonoma, 1984). Despite the significance of the implementation process, however, relatively little research attention has been directed to the area. Perhaps this is due to the tendency of some strategists to assume that shrewd strategy formulation is the only necessary elements for strategic success. In these cases, implementation is often viewed as a fairly mechanistic control function. In other words, implementation is treated by some managers and many scholars as a strategic afterthought. As expressed by Day and Wensley (1983),

> Many of the models of strategic management . . . tend to assume too simple a link between the development of strategic direction and its actual implementation via the allocation of resources. In practice, ... the actual process of resource allocation often incorporates a number of implicit but critical strategic moves (p. 86).

Our knowledge of the nature of strategy implementation and the reasons for its success or failure is limited (cf. Walker and Ruekert, 1987). Researchers interested in this area face a formidable challenge due to the general lack of existing research on which to base new efforts. The premise of this study is that a solid basis for implementation research does exist, although it requires a broadened perspective and the potential consideration of an eclectic collection of literature fields. Through a broadened treatment of the nature and roots of implementation, a foundation is revealed that will provide grounding for a variety of approaches to the study of strategy implementation. In the sections to follow, existing definitions and conceptualizations of implementation are first examined. These illustrate the wide array of perspectives that have been taken in the conceptualization and study of strategy implementation. Next, literature from a wide range of fields with implications for the study of implementation is considered. This is organized around a framework distinguishing between structural and interpersonal process views of the nature of implementation. Finally, thoughts on the state of implementation research and potential avenues for future work are presented.

The Nature of Implementation

One reason for the lack of a cohesive body of existing implementation research may he the diversity of perspectives that have been taken in defining the concept. The most common conceptualization has assumed implementation to be a relatively straightforward operationalization of a clearly articulated strategic plan (e.g., Wind and Robertson, 1983). Other researchers have taken different approaches such as emphasizing more interpersonal and behavioral elements (e.g., Cyert and March, 1963; Frankwick et al., 1994; Workman, 1993).

A review of the literature reveals few formal definitions of strategy implementation. Table 1 presents some of the different views that have been proposed.

Table 1. Perspectives on Implementation

- Implementation is a series of interventions concerning organizational structures, key personnel actions, and control systems designed to control performance with respect to desired ends. (Hrebiniak and Joyce, 1984)
- The implementation stage involves converting stratetic alternatives into an operating plan. (Aaker, 1988)
- Implementation is the managerial interventions that align organizational action with strategic intention. (Floyd and Woolridge, 1992)
- Implementation is the process that turns plans into action assignments and ensures that such assignments are executed in a manner that accomplishes the plan's stated objectives. (Kotler, 1984)
- Implementation is turning drawing board strategy into marketplace reality. (Bonoma, 1984)
- Implementation refers to the "how-to-do-it" aspects of marketing. Implementation deals with organizational issues, with the development of specific marketing programs and with the execution of programs in the field, (Cespedes. 1991)
- During the implementation phase, a policy decision must be spelled out in operational detail and resources allocated among programs. (Laffan, 1983)

The range of views put forth is considerable. One approach (e.g., Hrebiniak and Joyce, 1984) holds implementation to be an act of control and monitoring. This treatment of implementation as synonymous with control is a common perspective in many business strategy texts. Another common view (e.g., Floyd and Woolridge, 1992; Kotler, 1984) treats implementation as synonymous with execution of the strategic plan. This view is limited in that it fails to acknowledge the emergent nature of many implementation processes - initial plans are often adapted due to changing organizational or environmental conditions. Finally, several authors (e.g., Cespedes, 1991; Laffan, 1983) view implementation as a finer level of planning involving the allocation of resources and the resolution of operational issues. Combining several of these perspectives with more of a focus on the processes involved, strategy implementation is defined here as the communication, interpretation, adoption, and enactment of strategic plans. Next, a broad range of literature is reviewed that either directly addresses implementation issues or provides related insights that should be of interest to implementation researchers.

Implementation-related Research

A straightforward search for strategy implementation literature provides relatively little for the aspiring researcher. By taking a more broadened view, however, many meaningful insights can be found to guide new implementation research efforts. This section reviews a wide span of literature with implications and potentially valuable insights for the study of strategy implementation. The basic organizing framework for this review proposes that structural views and interpersonal process views are important general dimensions of strategy implementation (Skivington and Daft, 1991). Managers make adjustments to formal, structural elements of the organization such as roles, reporting relationships, and control mechanisms in order to enact strategic decisions. In addition to these formal factors, a range of interpersonal and cognitive factors may also become salient as managers strive to interpret and respond to a strategic initiative (cf. Skivington and Daft, 1991). In the sections below, literature from these areas is sampled, and implications for implementation research are highlighted.

Structural Views

Research taking a structural perspective has studied the effects of the formal organizational structure and control mechanisms on implementation processes and outcomes.

1. Organizational structure

Whereas extensive research has examined the relationship between strategy formulation and organizational structure (e.g., Bain, 1968; Miles and Snow, 1978; Porter, 1980), only limited attention has been given to the contingency between organizational structure and implementation processes. Gupta (1987) examined the relationships between SBUs' strategies, aspects of the corporate-SBU relationship, and implementation and found that structures that are more decentralized produce higher levels of SBU effectiveness, regardless of the strategic context. Drazin and Howard (1984) suggest that a proper strategy-structure alignment is a necessary precursor to the successful implementation of new business strategies. Changes in the competitive environment necessitate adjustments to the organizational structure. If the firm lags in making this realignment, they may exhibit poor performance and be at a serious competitive disadvantage.

2. Control mechanisms

A fundamental question facing managers is how to assess performance during and after the implementation of new strategy. This assessment or control function is a key aspect of implementation processes. Daft and Macintosh (1984) explore the role of formal control systems in strategy implementation. They define organizational control as a three-stage cycle including (1) planning a target or standard of performance; (2) monitoring or measuring activities designed to reach that target, and (3) implementing corrections if targets or standards are not being achieved. Both Jaworski and MacInnis (1989) and Jaworski et al. (1993) showed a strong relationship between the type of control system in use and firm performance. This implies that the nature of the control system in an implementation effort is a critical decision. It also suggests that control systems may need to be flexible in order to evolve as an implementation effort unfolds.

Interpersonal Process Views

Regardless of the nature of organizational structure and control systems in place, it seems clear that interpersonal processes and issues are an important part of any strategy implementation effort. In the next sections, research into strategic consensus, autonomous strategic behaviours, diffusionary processes, the effects of leadership and implementation styles, and communication and other interaction processes are considered.

1. Strategic consensus

The degree of strategic consensus between managers may influence the success with which strategic directives are implemented. Strategic consensus is a shared understanding and commitment to a strategic directive between individuals or groups within an organization. Whereas a general assumption in this literature has been that higher levels of consensus will lead to higher levels of firm performance, a more complex understanding of the nature and consequences of consensus has emerged. Other benefits of strategic consensus should be the development of a commitment among managers and a reduction of uncertainty in the organization. However, a negative consensus-performance relationship may result in highly complex and uncertain environments. In these environments, different organizational subunits need to respond to different external contingencies, requiring the maintenance of different belief structures to maximize effectiveness (Hrebiniak and Snow, 1982). In this environntent, the variance in perceptions and goals held by subunits may actually be beneficial to the firm.

Woolridge and Floyd (1989) explore the consensus construct further. They propose that scope – who is considered in evaluating consensus, and content – what decision-makers agree about, are important dimensions of consensus. Woolridge and Floyd also address another variable with important implications for implementation research, the extent to which managers are committed to the strategic initiative. As they describe, shared understanding without commitment may result in "counter effort" and negatively affect performance.

Consensus is an important factor in implementation-related decision making. In a study of the ancillary outcomes of group decision-making processes, Schweiger et al. (1989) found that groups of middle managers using dialectical inquiry and devil's advocacy approaches made significantly higher quality decisions than groups seeking total consensus in their decisions. This suggests that at least among peer groups of decision-makers, a certain amount of diversity of opinions may create a healthier environment that produces more effective strategic decisions. Total consensus may result in "group think" and the suppression of valuable individual opinions.

Whitney and Smith (1983) broaden the study of consensus to examine the interaction and belief differences between senior and middle managers. This topic is noteworthy as formulated plans are most typically passed to middle levels of the organization during the implementation process. Whitney and Smith propose that obtaining commitment to a strategic plan at all levels in the organization is often problematic. Operating managers may be apathetic in response to the planning efforts of upper management or may even perceive these efforts as a threat. The potential for conflict is further aggravated by the potential development of an *esprit de corps* within organizational groups. The authors found support for their belief that cohesiveness can result in greater polarization of organizational subgroups, thereby impeding the successful implementation of a strategic plan.

Taking an even broader view of strategic consensus, Nielsen (1983) contends that firms must achieve consensus both within and outside the firm in order to successfully implement business strategies. The firm's failure to at least "satisfice" (Kaufman, 1990) external constituencies such as regulatory agencies, environmentalist groups, and the like can seriously jeopardize an implementation effort if the constituency has the power to block or delay key elements of the strategy.

Finally, Floyd and Woolridge (1992) present a broad review of strategic consensus research. They propose that strategic consensus can be assessed along both cognitive and emotional dimensions. Cognitively, a lack of consensus is created by managers who don't share a common perception of the meaning of the strategy. This causes individuals to put forth efforts that are not always in harmony. Managers' affective consensus depends on how the proposed strategy fits with what managers perceive as the best interests of the organization and how it fits with managers' own self-interests. Both cognitive and affective consensus should be necessary for maximized organisational performance.

In sum, the strategic consensus literature provides a broad range of views of the value of a collective mind set during implementation efforts. The most common assumption of this research, a direct and positive relationship between consensus and firm performance, appears to be somewhat tenuous. More realistic appears to be the view that the consensus-performance relationship in implementation is moderated by numerous organizational and personal factors.

2. Autonomous strategic behaviors

When strategic consensus does not exist within the firm, organization members are not operating under the same goals and objectives. In this environment, managers may intentionally deviate from a strategic initiative in order to pursue their own desired ends. At times, this behavior may be well-intentioned as in the case of the manager who honestly feels that "her way" is best for the firm. At other times, however, deviation from a strategic initiative may be for self-serving purposes such as the protection of personal turf and power bases. In any case, these autonomous behaviors can have a profound effect on the success with which a strategic plan is implemented and the nature of the strategy that emerges. A body of research has examined these autonomous strategic behaviors and their antecedents and consequences.

Guth and MacMillan (1986) suggest that "self-interested interventions" on the part of middle managers are likely when their goals and beliefs are not highly congruent with those of senior management. Low personal commitment by middle managers may result in only passive compliance or, in a more extreme case, in "upward intervention" by middle managers during strategy formulation or implementation processes. Upward intervention may include subversive behaviors such as verbal arguments, objecting memos, coalition formation, the deliberate creation of barriers to implementation, and even outright sabotage. Passive intervention can take the form of giving the strategy of low priority or general "foot-dragging," both of which can result in unnecessary delays and inhibit the implementation effort. In an empirical study, Guth and MacMillan (1986) found that managers who believe their self-interest is being compromised can redirect a strategy, delay its implementation, reduce the quality of its implementation, and even totally sabotage the effort.

Connors and Romberg (1991) study the often subversive reactions of middle managers faced with a change in their power and authority base. The authors argue that the current trend toward flatter organizational structures has placed the true decision-making authority in the hands of line workers and the "coaching" function in the hands of senior management. In this environment, middle managers may feel their power bases slipping away and may behave subversively in an attempt to maintain their power and status. In a study of the implementation of a TQM program in a large firm, the authors find: (1) a strong desire on the part of middle managers to maintain the power and authority that traditionally separated them from the line workers: (2) several managers manipulating the program to their own best interests, particularly in cases where the strategic directives were ambiguous and left significant room for interpretation: and (3) an underlying suspicion among middle management that they were not being given full information by senior management. These findings may be particularly relevant in cases where the implementation of strategies requires significant organizational change.

A more positive view of autonomous behaviors is provided by Bonoma (1986). He feels that turbulent business environments require novel managerial responses. In his view, "subversives" are key individuals during these challenging periods. Subversives are "individuals who challenge old practices and when necessary, violate company rules and policy" (Bonoma, 1986, p. 113). These managers are able to improvise under conditions of change, are willing to change long-standing practices, and tend to be action-oriented. Bonoma makes the point that under many conditions a certain amount of autonomous strategic behaviour may be desirable.

3. Diffusion perspectives

One conceptualization of strategy implementation is as a "trickle down" process. In this view, senior management initiates strategies, which are then communicated through middle management to line workers. Whereas implementation processes may often be more iterative than this metaphor would suggest, the concept of diffusion is likely to be salient to many organizations and implementation processes. In this section, research on technology and organizational innovation diffusion is reviewed to provide insights into strategy implementation processes.

Diffusion research provides insights regarding strategy sponsors, adopters, firm-level factors, and the effects of the nature of the strategy being implemented. Robertson and Gatignon (1986) suggest that the reputation of the sponsoring senior executive is an important factor in facilitating organizational adoption. For adopters, research shows that outward thinkers are more apt to be early adopters (Robertson and Gatignon, 1986), and some organization members are naturally predisposed to adopt an innovation with little prodding, whereas others will wait for formal directives to adopt (Leonard-Barton and Deschamps, 1988). At the firm level, vertical communication patterns (Fidler and Johnson, 1984; Robertson and Gatignon, 1986), organizational inertia (Boecker, 1989), and the firm's overall strategic profile (Gaertner et al., 1984) may influence the rate of adoption of the new strategy within the organization. Finally, research in this area has suggested that the more radical the changes required by the implementation effort, the slower may be the rate of organizational adoption (Robertson and Gatignon, 1986).

4. *Leadership and implementation style.*

The leadership style of senior managers can have a significant effect on implementation elements such as the delegation of authority and decision-making. Gupta and Govindarajan (1984) address the relationship between the characteristics of an SBU's general manager and the perceptions of effectiveness in strategy implementation. The results of this interview-based study show that "build" SBU's should have general managers with greater marketing/sales experience, greater willingness to take risk, and greater tolerence for ambiguity than should "harvest" SBUs.

Nutt (1983) considers the link between the organizational climate (defined based on degrees of centralization, complexity, production, and efficiency) and various approaches to implementation. As he describes, the management of the implementation process generally requires a driving force in the organization in order to succeed. In some cases, implementation is driven by a change agent (or "champion") who is typically a high level leader who paves the way for plan adoption by shaping and guiding the planning process. Planner-managed processes involve the strategy's primary developer taking a leadership role in trying to "sell" the strategy. Finally, in participation-managed planning, organizational participants are involved in the strategy through a process of coopting. Another important dimension of implementation style is the technique used to enact the strategy. A unilateral approach requires the implementor to merely announce the plan and specify the behavior needed to comply. Manipulative techniques are more subtle, seeking to illuminate a problem and then steer users to new practices. Delegative techniques involve the coopting of those affected by the plan, seeking to involve them in the implementation process. A final dimension of implementation style considered by Nutt (1983) is the base of power used in the implementation process (reward, legitimate, referent, expert, or informational). The power base employed is closely tied to the technique used to guide implementation. In a later piece, Nutt (1986) suggests that managerial tactics and leadership style can play a critical role in overcoming the lower-level obstructionism that is prevalent to some extent in many implementation efforts. Line-level employees may use delay or prevent attempts toward change that they find particularly threatening or disagreeable.

Table 2. Summary of Conceptual Implementation-Related Literature

Article	Overview	Contribution
Nutt (1983)	This article takes the position that implementation prospects improve when the strategy planning process is linked to implementation when an implementation approach is tailored to fit the internal environment of an organization.	Considers a range of implementation techniques and power bases that, combined, form appropriate implementation approaches for a variety of planning situations (16 archetypical environments in all).
Nielsen (1983)	This article examines relationships between strategic planning and consensus building with external groups and constituencies. Methods for consensus building with external groups during strategic planning and implementation are discussed and five cases from different economic and political sectors are examined in conjunction with the principles considered.	Extends previous work which has considered internal consensus building by considering consensus building with external groups during strategic planning. Suggests consensus building with external groups will have a positive influence on both strategy development and implementation.
Drazin and Howard (1984)	New strategic objectives result from responses and a changing competitive environment. These changing strategies create administrative problems that require new or modified organisational design to support the strategy effectively. This study describes a general design technique that can be used to achieve a goal fit between strategic and design components, thus facilitating implementation and improving performance.	This article makes the case that strategy/structure realignment is a necessary precursor to strategy implementation. It presents a design process that allows organizational members to achieve this realignment.
Fidler and Johnson (1984)	The abilities of decision-makers to implement innovations at lower levels in the organization are crucial to organizational success. Risk and complexity are characteristics of innovations that can lead to resistance within the organization. Communication costs, types of power, and	The authors develop a series of propositions to explore the use of communication tactics to reduce the risk and complexity that inhibit the successful implementation of many new innovations within the organization.

Table 2 continued

Article	Overview	Contribution
	communication channels are structural characteristics that can be used by decision-makers to overcome the resistance. The interaction of these factors can determine the degree of successful innovations implemented within organizations.	
Bourgeois and Brodwin (1984)	The authors consider five process models of implementation (commander, change, collaborative, cultural and crescive). Two fundamental variables appear to characterize these different views, shifting continuously from the commander to the crescive model. They are, first, a shift from centralized to decentralized decision-making for both strategy development and implementation and, second, an increasing blurring of the distinction between "thinkers" and "doers".	Draws attention to an area (implementation) that has traditionally been treated as merely an activity following formulation. This article serves to synthesize advances in the study of implementation, structured around these five models.
Dess and Origer (1987)	This article makes a distinction and provides an overview of the two primary perspectives on consensus: consensus as either the outcome of a decision process and consensus as the process of building consensus. Several moderating factors in the relationship between consensus and performance are identified.	Presents an integrative model of the antecedents and consequences of consensus in strategy formulation.
Bonoma and Crittenden (1988)	Proposes a taxonomy relating structural variations and managerial skills to key issues in implementing marketing strategies. Developed through a series of in-depth interviews with high-level executives. The taxonomy was validated through a series of 44 case studies.	Raises several important issues related to implementation success. Notes the intertwined nature of strategy and implementation. Raises the interesting point that implementation structures and skills will influence the nature of the strategies that are formulated.

Table 2 continued

Article	Overview	Contribution
Hambrick and Cannella (1989)	The authors observed the following patterns of behaviour in cases of successful implementation: (1) Obtaining broad-based inputs and participation at the formulation stage; (2) carefully and deliberately assessing the obstacles to implementation; (3) making early use of the full array of implementation levers – resource commitments, subunit policies and programs, structure, people and rewards; (4) selling the strategy to everyone who matters (upward, downward, across and outward); (5) steadily fine tuning, adjusting, and responding as events and trends arise.	This article emphasises the importance of selling a strategy within the organization, an area that hasn't received much attention in previous implementation work.
Woolridge and Floyd (1989)	This article addresses the inconsistent findings that have been reported in exploring the link between consensus in the top management team and performance by providing a description of how the strategic process affects consensus. Synoptic and incremental processes are compared in terms of their effects on the scope, content, and degree of consensus. In addition, two dimensions of consensus, shared understanding and commitment, are considered.	Adds to the continuing debate on the relationship between consensus and performance by suggesting that the relationship between these two constructs is much more complex than previously hypothesized. Suggests several directions for future study.
Argyris (1989)	Presents the results of a group exercise designed to expose individual and organizational defensive routines based on the "Human Theory of Control".	The discussion of organizational defensive routines appears particularly salient as a means of explaining limitations in organizational learning and how these lead to harmful gaps and inconsistencies in the strategy process.

Table 2 continued

Article	Overview	Contribution
Priem (1990)	This article considers top management team competition, structure, and decision processes as well as environmental dynamism as antecedents to the consensus-performance relationship.	Since neither perfect disagreement (chaos) nor perfect agreement ("groupthink") are desirable within most top management teams, a curvilinear relationship is suggested between consensus and performance.
Sandy (1991)	Presents eight common breakdowns between strategy planning and implementation: (1) understanding the voice of the customer; (2) information is not organized for action; (3) the process of reaching conclusions does not involve the right people; (4) fragmented, piecemeal, or insufficient solutions; (5) no champions and few reasons to take on that task; (6) people you count on don't understand how to succeed; (7) nobody keeps score; and (8) nothing happens when you win.	Presents guidelines for successful implementation from a practitioner perspective. Several of the points (e.g., consideration of champions, differences in understanding) coincide with some of the more academic work in the area.
Floyd and Woolridge (1992)	This article examines an approach to implementation that focuses on the level of strategic understanding and commitment shared by managers within the organization. A framework identifying four categories of strategic consensus is introduced and used as the basic for analyzing differences in how managers perceive organizational priorities.	Describes a technique (consensus mapping) useful for identifying implementation gaps within an organization and identifies some techniques for closing those gaps.
Simkin (1996)	Focuses on the proper structuring of marketing planning processes to maximize the chances of successful implementation. Develops a list of planning pitfalls based on observational data.	Contends that an organized, ongoing program of guidance and control (or "policing") can overcome many problems encountered in planning and implementation. The benefits of this program are said to be communication, training, motivation, marketing intelligence and the achievement of a market orientation.

Table 3. Summary of Empirical Implementation-Related Literature

Study	Subjects/Research Method	Variables Studied	Analysis	Key Findings
Stagner (1969)	217 vice presidents and top executives from Fortune 500 companies; mailed questionnaire	(IV) Managerial cohesiveness, formality, centralization, satisfaction with process; (DV): Profitability (not used in examining relationships with managerial cohesiveness)	Correlation analysis	Positive correlation between executive satisfaction on decision-making process and profitability, supported view of corporation as a coalition; found three important dimensions of decision-making process; managerial cohesiveness, formality, and centralization.
Grinyer and Norburn (1977-78)	21 firms (91 executive respondents); field study with questionnaire	(IV) Existing objectives (who sets and influences), responsibility for marketing plans, nature and communication of information to senior management; (DV): Return on net assets	Correlation analysis	Higher financial performance is associated with the use of more information processes (channels of information); the use of informal channels is associated with high performance; no evidence to support the correlation between common perception of objectives and financial performance.
DeWoot, Heyvaert and Martou (1977-78)	123 firms; little information provided regarding research method or interviewees	(IV): Consensus, defined as agreement or means for innovation activities; (DV): Long-term profitability	Correlation analysis	Firm performance is not explained by the number of innovations made but its capacity for combining technical progress with corporate strategy and efficient decision-making.

Table 3 continued

Study	Subjects/Research Method	Variables Studied	Analysis	Key Findings
Bourgeois (1980)	On-site interviews with CEOs of 12 firms, field study with questionnaire completed by 67 top managers	(IV): Consensus on corporate goals (ends) and competitive strategies (means); (DV): Firm performance (composite measure)	Correlation analysis. ANOVA	Suggests that strategy makers should concentrate on reaching consensus concerning means (competitive strategies) rather than ends (goals) when formulating strategies for single-mission enterprises.
Hrebiniak and Snow (1982)	49 firms, 247 executive respondents, mailed questionnaire	(IV) Agreement on firm's strengths and weaknesses, environmental complexity; (DV): Return on assets	Partial correlations, factor analysis	Agreement among top managers is positively related to economic performance, even when controlling for other variables potentially related to organizational performance.
Whitney and Smith (1983)	90 student subjects; experimental design	(IV): Role (Product manager, strategic planner), cohesiveness level (control information cohesive); (DV): Attitude polarization and knowledge about the strategic plan	ANOVA	Suggests that cohesiveness can result in greater polarization, thereby impeding the successful implementation of the strategic plan.
Laffan (1983)	Four levels of actors involved in implementation of a public policy; field study approach	Communication control, (administrative, financial and political) and evaluation	General observations	The use of the "policy network" concept draws attention to the relationships that actors in the system must engage in to achieve their implementation goals.

Table 3 continued

Study	Subjects/Research Method	Variables Studied	Analysis	Key Findings
Gupta and Govindarajan (1984)	58 SBUs within eight Fortune 500 firms. Mailed survey instrument	(IV): Managerial characteristics; SBU strategy; (DV): Effectiveness at implementation	Regression	Suggest that "build" SBUs should, in general, have GMs with greater marketing/sales experience, greater willingness to take risk and greater tolerance for ambiguity than should "harvest" SBUs.
Gaertner, Gaertner and Akinnusi (1984)	Employees of two federal agencies; interviews (200), questionnaires (300) and archival data	Organizational context (mission, environmental support, competition and structure) and issues surrounding the innovation process	Primarily qualitative	Differences between agency types in attitudes toward the innovation were found: In the generalist organisation (EPA), the administrative innovation was sought by top management to improve coordination, but was difficult to achieve; in the specialist organization (MSHA), administrative innovation was more easily achieved but was less sought after.
Daft and MacIntosh (1984)	First stage: nine firms/31 respondents; Second stage: 20 firms/86 respondents; Unstruc-	Inductive identification and categorization of formal control systems	"Direct research" - qualitative exploration of central mechanisms in use	Two models are proposed: one links control systems to business level strategy implementation and the

Table 3 continued

Study	Subjects/Research Method	Variables Studied	Analysis	Key Findings
	tured and structured interviews			other defines primary and secondary roles for management control system components in the management control process.
DeRijcke, Faes and Vollering (1985)	Five purchasing cases	Decision variable differences between strategic and operational decisions	Decision systems analysis	The study found several differences between the decision processes involving strategic and operational decisions. For example, strategic and operational decision-making require different mixes of marketing stimuli.
Wernham (1985)	62 subjects at senior and middle management levels within the same firm, semi-structured interviews	None in particular, purely an inductive study examining emergent themes	Development of themes based on a qualitative study of three implementation efforts within the same organization	Factors influencing implementation were found to include: availability of resources of all kinds, top management support, perception of benefits, technical and organization validity, history of past implementation attempts, size of the implementing unit, and the nature of the market environment.

Table 3 continued

Study	Subjects/Research Method	Variables Studied	Analysis	Key Findings
Nutt (1986)	91 researcher-developed case studies; transactional path models and in-depth interviews	Tactical variables (tactics): Context variables (perceived importance, staff support, time pressure and process budgets); and an outcome variable (success rate)	ANOVA, correlation analysis, chi-squares analysis	Four general implementation tactics were used in 93 percent of cases (intervention, persuasion, participation, edict). Intervention tactics and their variations were effective for all types of changes and under varying levels of time pressure and importance, suggesting that managers should use these tactics more often.
Sproull and Hofmeister (1986)	School administrators (two levels) and elementary school teachers; Repeated measures design (four periods): Interviews and Likert scales	Elements of interpretation, attribution and inference	Simple comparison of mean responses	In the course of implementing the innovation some perceptions, attributions and inferences shifted over time but initial major differences associated with organizational position and commitment in the innovation did not change.
Guth and MacMillan (1986)	90 MBA students, 330 total incidents; Critical incident technique	Scope and success of strategy intervention	f-tests	Data suggest that middle managers who believe their self-interest is being compromised can redirect a strategy, delay or reduce the

Table 3 continued

Study	Subjects/Research Method	Variables Studied	Analysis	Key Findings
				quality of its implementation, or even totally sabotage the strategy.
Gupta (1987)	Eight firms, 58 senior executives and SBU senior managers; survey instrument	(IV): Strategic mission Competitive strategy. Openness of corporate SBU relations. Subjectivity in performance assessment, and corporate SBU decentralization; (DV): SBU's effectiveness multi-dimensional but primarily actual vs a priori expectations.	Regression analysis	For SBUs trying to build market share or to pursue differentiation as a competitive strategy, openness in corporate-SBU relations and subjectivity in performance assessment were found to be positively associated with effectiveness; for SBUs trying to maximize short-term earnings or to pursue low cost as a competitive strategy, the corresponding associations were found to be negative. In contrast, corporate-SBU decentralization emerged as positively associated with SBU's effectiveness irrespective of their strategic contexts.
Dess (1987)	19 firms, 74 top management team respondents; in-depth interviews and written questionnaires	(IV) Consensus on company objectives and competitive methods; (DV): Objective and subjective measures of firm performance	Correlation analysis	The results do not support the primary contention of the study: that consensus on both company objectives and competitive methods is

Table 3 continued

Study	Subjects/Research Method	Variables Studied	Analysis	Key Findings
				necessary to explain performance differences between firms but, rather, consensus on either is positively related to organizational performance. The results also suggest that reaching consensus on both of these areas provides no performance advantage over reaching consensus in just one of these areas.
Leonard-Barton and Deschamps (1988)	93 salespeople for a single computer manufacturer, telephone survey	(IV) Management influence, personal characteristics and skills of targeted users, social influence (DV): Measure of use (control variables); Physical accessibility and training	Hierarchical regression	Employees whose characteristics incline them to adopt an innovation will do so without management support or urging if it is simply made available. Employees low on these characteristics will await a managerial directive before adopting.
Govindarajan (1988)	Executives and general managers at 24 Fortune 500 firms; mailed survey instrument	(IV): Measures of competitive strategy budget evaluative style, locus of control, and decentralization; (DV): SBU effectiveness	Bivariate regression and systems approaches to fit	Findings suggest that matching key administrative mechanisms (org. structure, control systems, and managers' characteristics) with the firm's strategic locus (low cost/differentiation) will be

Table 3 continued

Study	Subjects/Research Method	Variables Studied	Analysis	Key Findings
				associated with superior performance. All three mechanisms were found to be important in achieving effective implementation.
Boecker (1989)	51 semiconductor firms: Interviews, archival data	(IV): Current strategy, initial strategy, distribution of functional influence, organizational age, entrepreneur's tenure, management ownership; (DV): performance (sales increase relative to industry)	Correlation and regression analysis	Characteristics of an organization's founding imprint its initial strategy by contributing to an internal consensus around a given strategic approach. Conditions subsequent to founding also influence the degree to which an initial strategy is perpetuated.
Schweiger, Sandberg and Rechner (1989)	120 middle and upper-middle-level managers, experimental design	(IV): Subjects used either a dialectical inquiry, devil's advocacy, or consensus approach to developing case analysis recommendations; (DV): Group performance, group meeting time, and group members' reactions	ANOVA	Compared to consensus groups, groups using dialectical inquiry and devil's advocacy made significantly higher quality decisions. There were no differences between dialectical inquiry and devil's advocacy groups. Experience in using the three decision-making approaches improved decision quality, critical reevaluation levels and the

Table 3 continued

Study	Subjects/Research Method	Variables Studied	Analysis	Key Findings
				reactions of group members and reduced time required to reach decisions.
Johnson and Frohman (1989)	3 firms; Field study	Unspecified variables related to implementation and middle management perceptual "gaps"	General obser-vations only	Suggest several adaptive organizational responses to eliminate middle management gaps. These include redefining jobs and rewards to legitimize the integrating function of middle manag-ers giving individuals and teams authority, holding them accountable, getting middle managers the information they need and helping people in the middle build lateral networks.
Nutt (1990)	79 executives and 89 middle managers; Controlled simulation	(IV): Decision styles; (DV): Prospect of adoption and perceived risk; (control variables): age, experience, and educational background. Group differences also considered.	ANOVA and repeated measures techniques	Views of both adoption and risk were found to be influenced by decision style. The decisions of top execu-tives were more style depen-dent than those of middle managers. Several differences were found in decision-making based on the extended Jungian decision style framework used.

Table 3 continued

Study	Subjects/Research Method	Variables Studied	Analysis	Key Findings
Woolridge and Floyd (1990)	20 firms (156 respondents): semi-structured interviews and questionnaire	(IV): Involvement in the strategy process, consensus (commitment and understandings); (DV): organizational performance (subjective assessment)	Correlations, partial correlations, qualitative findings	The results suggest that involvement in the formation of strategy is associated with improved organizational performance. Strategic consensus among middle-level managers is related to involvement in the strategic process but not to organizational performance.
Pinto and Prescott (1990)	408 project managers from a broad range of firms; mail survey	(IV): Project implementation profile (increases key success factors in implementation), stage of project life cycle; (DV): perceived project success	Regression, factor analysis	The relative importance of planning and tactical factors is contingent upon the type of success measure employed.
Skivington and Daft (1991)	57 strategic decisions; combination of open-ended interviews and closed-end survey instrument based on critical, incident technique	Elements of structure, systems, interaction, and sanctions	Partial correlations and cluster analysis	Implementation utilized both structural framework and interaction process elements, but a different implementation gestalt characterized each type of strategic decision.
St. John and Rue (1991)	15 carpet industry firms (165 total respondents); mail survey	(IV): Consensus on competitive strengths and company goals, frequency of	Chi-square, correlation analysis	Findings showed that those firms that made more frequent use of planning

Table 3 continued

Study	Subjects/Research Method	Variables Studied	Analysis	Key Findings
		use of coordinating mechanisms; (DV): out-standing performance" on dimensions of style, quality, and service		techniques experienced higher levels of interdepart-mental consensus. Consensus between departments was strongly related to marketplace performance reputation.
Connors and Romberg (1991)	A single manufacturer (600 employees); ethnography	Middle and lower management strategies for obstructing TQM implementation	General observations	(1) Desire to maintain power and authority caused middle managers to be slow to transfer decision-making authority to lower level workers; (2) In situations where policy objectives were ambiguous, managers manipulated the program to their own advantage; and (3) Middle management felt they were not being given full information by senior management.
Dopson, Risk and Stewart (1992)	Senior and middle managers in 12 firms; in-depth interviews	Changes affecting middle managers' jobs, how their jobs have changed, and the implications managers see for their work, career and life	General observations	Whether middle managers see change as positive or negative seems to depend on: (1) How clear the need for change is within the

Table 3 *continued*

Study	Subjects/Research Method	Variables Studied	Analysis	Key Findings
				organization; (2) The extent to which change is seen as normal; (3) What is done to try to help managers think positively and adapt to change; and (4) Whether the managers see themselves primarily as professionals or primarily as managers.
Floyd and Woolridge (1992)	MBA students conducted in-depth field studies of their own firms (25 firms total); survey instrument	Middle manager role (of four in typology) organizational strategy	Factor analysis; MANOVA	This study builds a typology of four middle management strategic roles (championing alternatives, synthesizing information, facilitating adaptability, and implementing deliberate strategy). Weak support is found for a prior hypotheses.
Bryson and Bromiley (1993)	68 case descriptions of major strategies; variables of interest were coded using information in cases	(IV): Context of the strategy planning and implementation processes; (DV): Strategy outcomes	Factor analysis and regression	A number of contextual variables strongly influence aspects of the strategy planning and implementation process and, thus, indirectly influence strategy outcomes.

Table 3 continued

Study	Subjects/Research Method	Variables Studied	Analysis	Key Findings
Schwenk and Cosier (1993)	152 student subjects; experimental design	(IV): Three treatment conditions (devil's advocacy, agreement, control), subsets of high and low consensus; (DV): Performance (as evaluated by independent judges)	ANOVA	The results of this experiment suggest that the overall effects of consensus on decision-making are positive. Further, the results suggest that structuring top management teams to achieve consensus on objectives may improve their performance. Other results suggest the devil's advocacy technique may lead to better performance in individual decisions but may damage group morale.
Egelhoff (1993)	Senior management members within each of eight U.S. and eight Japanese semi-conductor firms (number of participants not specified); in-depth structured and semi-structured interviews	Unique product/market advantage, withdrawal decisions, role of process technology, success of process technology, and the importance of vertical integration	Consideration of emergent themes and differences between "strategy-oriented" U.S. firms and "implementation-oriented" Japanese firms	Several advantages and disadvantages of competing through strategy implementation (rather than through superior strategy) are considered. For example, in implementation-oriented environments fewer different strategies exist, producing more direct competition and a greater emphasis on quality and cost.

Study	Subjects/Research Method	Variables Studied	Analysis	Key Findings
Lamont, Williams and Hoffman (1994)	76 firms pursuing three diversification strategies (vertical, related, unrelated)	(IV): Strategy implementation speech; (DV): Performance change during transition, recovery time	ANCOVA, LIFEREG	This study examined firm performance deterioration during reorganization periods and the time required for performance to recover to prereorganization levels. Prior strategy and implementation speed were found to affect both transition performance and recovery time.
Waldersee and Sheather (1996)	35 mid- to upper-level managers	Multiple case study simulation methods with measures of leadership styles, involvement in the change process, locus of control, risk aversion	f-tests	Examined the effects of strategy on leader behavior and choice of implementation actions. Results show that strategic context influences managers' implementation intentions.
Strahle, Spiro, and Acito (1996)	25 chief executives at consumer grocery product firms; 367 sales managers	Marketing strategy categorization, product life cycle dimension, sales objective categorization	Nonparametric sign test, z-test of differences, f-tests	The results show that there are often differences between marketing executives and their sales managers concerning specific product strategies. Emphasizes the need for input and cooperation from all constituencies involved in marketing a product for successful implementation.

In a widely cited piece, Bourgeois and Brodwin (1984) consider five general leadership styles in strategy implementation. These models all encompass elements of both strategy formulation and implementation as well as general, culture-like characteristics of the firm. The commander model is closest to the traditional strategy literature in its focus on centralized direction from the CEO to guide the firm's strategy. The change model emphasizes how organizational structure, incentive compensation, control systems, and other factors can be used to facilitate the implementation of a somewhat radical new strategy. The collaborative model focuses on group decision-making and negotiated outcomes for the firm. The cultural model is closely tied to work on organizational culture (e.g., Deshpande and Webster, 1989) and suggests that lower level employees can be infused with a strong set of collective values, which allows them to participate in the strategic thinking and implementation efforts of the firm. Finally, the crescive model suggests that middle managers should be responsible for a great degree of development, championing, and implementation of new strategies. A fundamental element of the crescive model is the shifting of decision-making and implementation authority to lower levels in the organization than in any of the other models. The Bourgeois and Brodwin (1984) typology illustrates the significant differences in implementation style that exist and may be used in different organizations.

Taking a slightly different perspective, Redding and Catalanello (1994) propose an "improvisational" approach to implementing strategic change in an organization. This view is based on the belief that "most organizational change results not from plans and fixed programs for change but from ... the collective learning of entire organizations" (p. xi). This improvisational approach consists of three major components (1) encouraging experimentation, grass roots initiatives and championing; (2) directing change by sanctioning without taking over, quietly clearing away obstacles, and facilitating cross-fertilization; and (3) recognizing, rewarding and institutionalizing change through changes in formal structures, rewards policies, etc. In this view, leadership style can create an environment that is highly conducive to successful strategy implementation efforts.

5. Communication and interaction processes.

The interaction and communication between managers and coalitions of managers is perhaps the most significant informal process within most organizations (Workman, 1993). Thus, research in this area may explicate some of the major reasons for the success or failure of implementation efforts. Hambrick and Cannella (1989) stress the importance of both vertical and lateral interaction in implementation processes. Their guidelines for successful strategy implementation include: (1) obtaining broad-based inputs and organizational participation at the strategy formulation stage; (2) assessing in advance the potential obstacles to implementation; (3) making early and decisive moves in important areas such as resource commitments, organizational structure, and reward mechanisms; (4) "selling" the strategy to all affected organizational members, both vertically and laterally; and (5) fine tuning, adjusting, and responding as events and trends arise. Sandy (1991) supports many of these views and adds that breakdowns in implementation occur when the strategic initiative is not well organized for action, that is, when necessary implementation behaviors are not well specified. This can cause key organization members to fail in implementation simply because they do not understand how to succeed.

Argyris (1989) notes the significance of organizational defensive routines and considers their implications for strategy implementation. He proposes that defensive routines exist in virtually all organizations. These routines limit learning and often lead to perceptual gaps and other differences in understanding between organizational members. These differences can hamper implementation efforts. Some of the defensive routines considered include "going along" with a higher level executive despite personal beliefs to the contrary, failing to understand what issues may be discussed with senior management, and withholding objections to a strategy until it reaches the active implementation stage. Argyris (1989) suggests that firms must work actively to eliminate these defensive routines if they hope to successfully implement strategic efforts.

Summary

Strategy implementation is a multifaceted and complex organizational process. As such, a wide range of related research areas may have worthwhile implications for its study. In the preceding sections, a broad base of literature was briefly reviewed to suggest areas with potentially valuable insights for implementation researchers. These and other articles are summarized in Tables 2 and 3, which highlight conceptual and empirical implementation-related research respectively.

The State of Implementation Research

Despite the diverse nature of the literature reviewed, there are some consistent findings that are worth highlighting. First, several views of the nature of the implementation process were presented. Implementation is a complex phenomenon, including elements such as internal and external resource negotiation (Day and Wensley, 1983), political processes such as jockeying for influence (Frankwick et al., 1994), and a shaping and adoption process at multiple levels in the organization (Laffan, 1983; Leonard-Barton and Deschamps, 1988). Although not addressed extensively in this review, it also appears clear that strategy formulation and implementation are intertwined processes with success in both necessary for superior firm performance (Bonoma, 1984; Cespedes, 1991).

Several issues related to the managers implementing the strategy emerged. Managers may engage in self-interested (or "subversive") behaviors, at times to the detriment of the implementation effort (Connors and Romberg, 1991; Guth and MacMillan, 1986). In certain environments, however, a degree of this "maverick" behavior may be desirable as it breaks established organizational routines (Bonoma, 1986). In a related area, the degree of strategic consensus among managers that breeds implementation success appears to be moderated by several factors related to the strategy being implemented and the organizational environment (Priem, 1990; Schweiger et al., 1989). Achieving consensus with key constituents outside the firm may also be important for implementation success (Bourgeois, 1980).

Finally, several key factors influencing potential implementation success emerged. Early involvement in the strategy process by a wide and deep range of organizational members appears to be a predictor of implementation success (Hambrick and Cannella, 1989; Sandy, 1991). In part, this early involvement may serve to reduce the perceptual gaps that exist in an organization regarding a new strategy (Johnson and Frohman, 1989; Wernham, 1985). It seems clear that the most successful implementing organizations must be fairly fluid in their ability to adapt to changing environmental conditions and new strategies. This fluidity is manifest in their ability to adjust organizational structures (Drazin and Howard, 1984; Ruekert, Walker. and Roering, 1985), leadership style, and culture (Bourgeois and

Brodwin, 1984; Gupta and Govindarajan, 1984: Nutt, 1983) to better meet new strategic realities. In all, a broad examination of implementation-related literature reveals a somewhat fragmented yet insightful body of work. An advantage of this broad grounding is that it offers many opportunities for further strategy implementation research.

Future Implementation Research

It is clear that well-conceived strategies have little value unless they are effectively implemented. Thus, implementation should be a topic of high interest to both managers and strategy researchers. As has been noted, relatively little direct research attention has been given to the area, although that appears to be changing to some extent. It seems that strategy implementation is a fertile area for future study. There are numerous forms which these future efforts might take.

First, while the formulation aspect of strategy is most often in the domain of senior managers, implementation appears much more closely tied to the daily activities of middle management. Thus, if we are to improve our understanding of the process and key success factors involved in implementation, it appears essential to better understand the daily lives of middle managers. Ethnographic-type research (e.g., Frankwick et al. 1994; Workman, 1993) has provided valuable insights into strategy processes in the past and should be pursued to better understand factors influencing strategy implementation and middle managers.

Second, it seems clear that aspects of the firm such as culture, organizational structure, and management style may have a profound effect on implementation processes. More research is needed on the influence of these firm factors on strategy implementation success. For this type of study, a more broad-based, cross-sectional approach would be effective. For example, firms could self-categorize their corporate culture based on a profile instrument. Firms of different cultural orientations can then be measured in terms of implementation effectiveness, while perhaps also controlling for other salient factors like industry effects and firm size.

More study needs to be done to identify the key factors that influence individual-level commitment, performance, and success in strategy implementation. Virtually all prior implementation research has examined factors and outcomes at the organizational level. A managerial-level view of implementation may provide valuable insights into factors, heretofore overlooked, that influence overall implementation success. Sampling is often a challenge in this form of research. Whereas mailing lists of high-level executives are available and the group is reasonably accessible through mass mailings, the middle manager is much more difficult to target, particularly when pursuing a multi-firm, cross-sectional approach.

There is also a great need for validated measures of many of the constructs that have been identified as influencing strategy implementation. The development of measures for concepts such as middle manager involvement in the strategy, autonomy in implementation, and the "newness" of the strategy for the organization would advance the field dramatically. There are currently not enough of such tools available to the implementation researcher.

Finally, whereas implementation research may benefit from the different perspectives offered in its eclectic roots, there is a significant need for detailed and comprehensive conceptual models related to strategy implementation. To date, implementation research has been fairly fragmented due to the lack of clear models on which to build. If the area is to advance, more conceptual efforts must be made to enable strategy implementation to achieve an identity of its own as a valid and distinguishable area of study.

In general, it is hoped that this background work will serve to further the study of strategy implementation processes. Implementation is an essential piece in the formula for success of any business. Effectiveness in implementation can even serve as a source of competitive advantage in industries where unique ideas and strategies are difficult to achieve. Although it has long been recognized that the majority of failed strategies break down in the implementation phase, researchers and practitioners have little concrete knowledge of this area. Some of the reasons for our lack of knowledge in this area are the difficulties found gaining insights into the inner workings of a firm, weak definitions of the construct itself, and the lack of a cohesive base of knowledge on which to build additional research efforts. This article has attempted to address the latter two points with the hope of precipitating further study of this important topic.

The author is grateful to Michael P. Mokwa for his guidance in the development of this manuscript.

References

1. Aaker, David A. *Strategic Market Management,* 2nd ed., Wiley & Sons, New York. 1988.
2. Argyris, Chris: Strategy Implementation: An Experience in Learning. *Organizational Dynamics* **18** (Autumn 1989): 4–15.
3. Bain, J. S.: *Industrial Organization,* 2nd ed., Wiley & Sons, New York. 1968.
4. Boecker, Warren: Strategic Change: The Effects of Founding and History. *Academy of Management Journal* **32** (1989): 489–515.
5. Bonoma, Thomas V.: Making Your Marketing Strategies Work. *Harvard Business Review* **62** (March/April 1984): 69–76.
6. Bonoma, Thomas V.: Marketing Subversives. *Harvard Business Review* **64** (November/December 1986): 113–118.
7. Bonoma, Thomas V., and Crittenden, Victoria L.: Managing Marketing Implementation. *Sloan Management Review* **29** (1988): 7–14.
8. Bourgeois, L.J.: Performance and Consensus. *Strategic Management Journal* **1** (July—September 1980): 227–248.
9. Bourgeois, L.J., and Brodwin, David R.: Strategic Implementation: Five Approaches to an Elusive Phenomenon. *Strategic Management Journal* **5** (1984): 241–264.
10. Bryson, John M., and Bromiley, Philip: Critical Factors Affecting the Planning and Implementation of Major Projects. *Strategic Management Journal* **14** (1993): 319–337.
11. Cespedes, Frank V.: *Organizing and Implementing the Marketing Effort,* Addison-Wesley Publishing. Reading, MA. 1991.
12. Connors, Jeanne L. and Romberg, Thomas A.: Middle Management and Quality Control Strategies for Obstuctionism. *Human Organization* **50** (1991): 61-65.
13. Cyert, Richard M., and March, James G.: *A Behavioural Theory of the Firm.* Prentice-Hall, Englewood Cliffs, NJ. 1963.
14. Daft, Richard L., and MacIntosh, Norman B.: The Nature and Use of Formal Control Systems for Management Control and Strategy Implementation. *Journal of Management* **10** (1984): 42.
15. Day, George S., and Wensley, Robin. Marketing Theory with a Strategic Orientation. *Journal of Marketing* **47** (Fall 1983): 78-89.
16. DeRijcke, Jacques, Faes, Wouter, and Vollering, Jan.: Strategy Formulation and Implementation during Purchasing of Production Materials. *Journal of Business Research* **13** (1985): 19-33.

17. Deshpande, Rohit, and Webster, Frederick E. Jr.: Organizational Culture and Marketing. Defining the Research Agenda. *Journal of Marketing* **53** (January 1989): 3-15.

18. Dess, Gregory G.: Consensus on Strategy Formulation and Organizational Performance: Competitors in a Fragmented Industry. *Strategic Management Journal* **8** (1987): 259-277.

19. Dess, Gregory G., and Origer, Nancy K.: Environment, Structure, and Consensus in Strategy Formulation: A Conceptual Integration. *Academy of Management Review* **12** (1987): 3 13–330.

20. DeWoot, P., Heyvaert, H., and Martou, F.: Strategic Management: An Empirical Study of 168 Belgian Firms. *International Studies of Management and Organization* **7** (Winter 1977–78): 60–75.

21. Dopson, Sue, Risk, Anne, and Stewart, Rosemary: The Changing Role of the Middle Manager in the United Kingdom. *International Studies of Management and Organization* **22** (1992): 40–53.

22. Drazin, Robert, and Howard, Peter: Strategy Implementation: A Technique for Organizational Design. *Columbia Journal of World Business* **19** (Summer 1984): 40–46.

23. Egelhoff, William G.: Great Strategy or Great Strategy Implementation–Two Ways of Competing in Global Markets. *Sloan Management Review* **34** (Winter 1993): 37–50.

24. Fidler, Lori A., and Johnson, J. David: Communication and Innovation Implementation. *Academy of Management Review* **9** (1984): 704–7 11.

25. Floyd, Steven W., and Woolridge, Bill: Managing Strategic Consensus: The Foundation of Effective Implementation. *Academy of Management Executive* **6** (1992); 27–39.

26. Frankwick, Gary L., Ward, James C., Hutt, Michael D., and Reingen, Peter H.: Evolving Patterns of Organizational Beliefs in the Formation of Strategy. *Journal of Marketing* **58** (April 1994): 96–110.

27. Gaertner, Gregory H., Gaertner, Karen N., and Akinnusi, David M.: Environment, Strategy, and the Implementation of Administrative Change: The Case of Civil Service Reform. *Academy of Management Journal* **27** (1984); 525–543.

28. Govindarajan, Vijay.: A Contingency Approach to Strategy Implementation at the Business Unit Level: Integrating Administrative Mechanisms with Strategy. *Academy of Management Journal* **31** (4) (1988): 828-853.

29. Grinyer, P., and Norburn, D.: Planning for Existing Markets: An Empirical Study. *International Studies of Management and Organization* **7** (Winter 1977–78); 99–122.

30. Gupta, Anil K.: SBU Strategies, Corporate-SBU Relations, and SBU Effectiveness in Strategy Implementation. *Academy of Management Journal* **30** (1987); 477–500.

31. Gupta, Anil K., and Govindarajan, Vijay: Business Unit Strategy: Managerial Characteristics, and Business Unit Effectiveness at Strategy Implementation. *Academy of Management Journal* **27** (1984): 25–41.

32. Guth, William D., and MacMillan, Ian.: Strategic Implementation versus Middle Management Self-Interest. *Strategic Management Journal* **7** (1986): 313-337.

33. Hambrick, Donald C., and Cannella, Albert A. Jr.: Strategy Implementation as Substance and Selling. *Academy of Management Executive* **3** (November 1989): 278-285.

34. Hrebiniak, L. and Joyce, W.F.: *Implementing strategy*, Macmillan, New York, 1984.

35. Hrebiniak, L., and Snow, C.C.: Top Management Agreement and Organizational Performance. *Human Relations* **35** (December 1982): 1139-1158.

36. Jaworski, Bernard J., and MacInnis, Deborah J.: Marketing Jobs and Management Controls: Toward a Framework. *Journal of Marketing Research* **26** (November 1989): 406-419.

37. Jaworski, Bernard J., Stathakopoulos, Vlasis, and Krishnan, H. Shanker.: Control Combinations in Marketing: Conceptual Framework and Empirical Evidence. *Journal of Marketing* **57** (January 1993): 57-69.

38. Johnson, Leonard L., and Frohman, Alan L.: Identifying and Closing the Gap in the Middle of Organizations. *Academy of Management Executive* **3** (1989): 107–114.

39. Kaufman, Bruce E.: A New Theory of Satisficing. *Journal of Behavioral Economics* 19 (1990): 35.

40. Kotler, Philip: *Marketing Management: Analysis, Planning, and Control,* 5th ed., Prentice-Hall, Englewood Cliffs, NJ. 1984.

41. Laffan, Brigid.: Policy Implementation in the European Community: The European Social Fund as a Case Study. *Journal of Common Market Studies* **21**(1983): 389–408.

42. Lamont, Bruce T., Williams, Robert J., and Hoffman, James J.: Performance during "M-Form" Reorganization and Recovery Time: The Effects of Prior Strategy and Implementation Speed. *Academy of Management Journal* **37** (1994): 153–166.

43. Leonard-Barton, Dorothy, and Deschamps, Isabelle.: Managerial Influence in the Implementation of New Technology. *Management Science* **34** (1988): 1252–1265.

44. Miles, Raymond E., and Snow, Charles C.: *Organizational Strategy, Structure, and Process,* McGraw-Hill, New York. 1978.

45. Nielsen, Richard P.: Strategic Planning and Consensus Building for External Relations–Five Cases. *Long Range Planning* **16** (1983); 74–81.

46. Nutt, Paul C.: Implementation Approaches for Project Planning. *Academy of Management Review* **8** (1983); 600–611.

47. Nutt, Paul C.: Tactics of Implementation. *Academy of Management Journal* **29** (1986): 230–261.

48. Nutt. Paul C.; Strategic Decisions Made by Top Executives and Middle Managers with Data and Process Dominant Styles. *Journal of Management Studies* **27** (1990): 173–194.

49. Pinto, Jeffrey K., and Prescott, John E.: Planning and Tactical Factors in the Project Implementation Process. *Journal of Management Studies* **27** (1990): 305–327.

50. Porter, Michael E.: *Competitive Strategy: Techniques for Analyzing Industries and Competitors.* The Free Press, New York. 1980.

51. Priem, Richard L.: Top Management Team Group Factors, Consensus and Firm Performance. *Strategic Management Journal* **11** (1990): 469-478.

52. Redding, John C., and Catalanello, Ralph C.: *Strategic Readiness.* Jossey-Bass, San Francisco, 1994.

53. Robertson, Thomas S., and Gatignon, Hubert.: Competitive Effects on Technology Diffusion. *Journal of Marketing* **50** (July 1986): 1-12

54. Ruekert, Robert W., Walker, Orville C, Jr., and Roering, Kenneth J.: The Organization of Marketing Activities: A Contingency Theory of Structure and Performance. *Journal of Marketing* **49** (1985): 13-25.

55. Sandy, William.: Avoid the Breakdown between Planning and Implementation. *Journal of Business Strategy* **12** (September/October 1991): 30-33.

56. Schweiger, David M., Sandberg, William R., and Rechner, Paula L.: Experiential Effects of Dialectical Inquiry, Devil's Advocacy, and Consensus Approaches to Strategic Decision Making. *Academy of Management Journal* **32** (1989): 745–772.

57. Schwenk, Charles R., and Cosier, Richard A.: Effects of Consensus and Devil's Advocacy on Strategic Decision-Making. *Journal of Applied Social Psychology* **23** (1993): 126–139.

58. Simkin, Lyndon: People and Processes in Marketing Planning: The Benefits of Controlling Implementation. *Journal of Marketing Management* **12** (1996): 375–390.

59. Skivington, James E., and Daft, Richard L.: A Study of Organizational "Framework" and "Process" Modalities for the Implementation of Business-Level Strategic Decisions. *Journal of Management Studies* **28** (1991): 45–68.

60. Sproull, Lee S., and Hofmeister, Kay Ramsay.: Thinking about Implementation. *Journal of Management* **12 (1)** (1986); 43–60.

61. Stagner, R.: Corporate Decision Making; An Empirical Study. *Journal of Applied Psychology* **53** (February 1969): 1–13.

62. St. John, Caron H., and Rue, Leslie W.: Research Notes and Communications: Coordinating Mechanisms, Consensus between Marketing and Manufacturing Groups and Marketplace Performance. *Strategic Management Journal* **12** (1991): 549–555.

63. Strahle, William M., Spiro, Rosann L., and Acito, Frank: Marketing and Sales: Strategic Alignment and Functional Implementation. *Journal of Personal Selling & Sales Management* **16** (1996): 1–18.

63. Waldersee, Robert, and Sheather, Simon: The Effects of Strategy Type on Strategy Implementation Actions. *Human Relations* **49** (1996); 105–122.

64. Walker, Orville C., and Ruekert, Robert W.: Marketing's Role in the Implementation of Business Strategies; A Critical Review and Conceptual Framework. *Journal of Marketing* **51** (July 1987): 15–33.

65. Wernham, Roy.: Obstacles to Strategy Implementation in a Nationalized Industry. *Journal of Management Studies* **22** (1985): 633–648.

66. Whitney. J. C., and Smith, R.A.: Effects of Group Cohesiveness on Attitude Polarization and the Acquisitions of Knowledge in a Strategic Planning Context. *Journal of Marketing Research* **20** (May 1983): 167–176.

67. Wind, Yoram, and Floyd, Steven W.: The Strategy Process: Middle Management Involvement and Organizational Performance. *Strategic Management Journal* **11** (1990): 231–241.

68. Wind, Yoram, and Robertson, Thomas S.: Marketing Strategy: New Directions for Theory and Research. *Journal of Marketing* **47** (Spring 1983): 12–25.

69. Woolridge, Bill, and Floyd, Steven W.: Research Notes and Communications: Strategic Process Effects on Consensus. *Strategic Management Journal* **10** (1989): 295–302.

70. Workman, John P. Jr.: Marketing's Limited Role in New Product Development in One Computer Systems Firm. *Journal of Marketing Research* **30** (November 1993): 405–421.

Total Business Strategy – The Missing Link

Eli Noy

Eli Noy is a Lecturer in Business Strategy & Management Controls, Recanati School of Business Administration, Tel-Aviv University, Israel.

Source: *Long Range Planning,* Vol. 31, No. 6, 1998, pp. 927-932.

> '*Total Business Strategy'* is the missing link between the aloof 'Mission State-ment' and the particular 'Functional Strategies', that will make strategy formula-tion more implementation oriented. *Total Business Strategy* addresses five strategic questions:
>
> 1. What are our markets? What are the needs (existing or to be developed) of the markets and customers that our firm wants to satisfy?
> 2. What should be our 'generic' competitive advantage?
> 3. Are we going to be technology leaders or followers?
> 4. What is our attitude to risk? What risks, and to what extent are we willing to take?
> 5. What are our long range quantitative targets?

What is Strategy?

Managers of Strategic Business Units (SBUs) who formulate a strategy for their business are faced with the questions: "What is Strategy?" and "What decisions should manage-ment take to define a workable Total Business Strategy which will guide functional man-agers in formulating their own strategy in line with the Total Business Strategy?" Manag-ers look for articles and books published on this subject, the closest they will be able to find is the 'Mission Statement' (or 'Vision') and 'Sustainable Competitive Advantage' but without giving an operational management-oriented answer.

Michael Porter states that "A company can outperform rivals only if it can establish a difference that it can preserve" and "The essence of strategy is choosing to perform activi-ties differently than rivals do."[14] Porter's view, strategy is sustainable competitive advan-tage, a theme he pursues in *Competitive Strategy*[11] and *Competitive Advantage.*[12] He defines the "determinants of firm success" as follows:[13]

1. The company must develop and implement an internally consistent set of goals and functional policies that collectively define its position in the market.

2. This internally consistent set of goals and policies aligns the firm's strengths and weaknesses with the external (industry) opportunities and threats.
3. The firm's strategy must be centrally concerned with the creation and exploitation of its so-called 'distinctive competencies'.

Gary Hamel, in an interview with the editor of the *European Management Journal*,[5] defines his approach to strategy in the three ways companies compete by

*   building core competencies.
*   building a worldwide distribution and brand infrastructure.
*   creating product disciplines.

Peter Pekar, Jr. and Stan Abraham in their article "Is Strategic Management Living Up to Its Promise?"[10] define the best practice Strategic Management Stage Activities, as found in their research:

*   strategic focus
*   financial position
*   core capabilities
*   opportunity definition
*   risk assessment
*   value impact
*   stakeholders assessment
*   opportunity development
*   operating policy

Fred R. David[4] defines 'Strategy Formulation' as consisting of three parts:

1. develop mission statement
2. establish long-term objectives
3. generate, evaluate and select strategies

while part of the 'Implementation Process' is the development of functional strategies. Most text books on strategy have an attitude similar to David's and consider the Mission Statement as containing all necessary building blocks of the definition of 'Strategy'. In all these articles, as well as in many others, *managers cannot find an agreed and consistent answer to their need for a workable definition of Strategy.*

The Mission Statement

Collins and Porras in *Built to Last*[2] found in their research that

> ... , the fundamental distinguishing characteristic of the most enduring and successful corporations is that they preserve a cherished core ideology ...

which together with an "envisioned future" constitutes the 'Vision'. Not all companies have 'visions' or 'mission statements', and if they do, the scope varies significantly. Most mission statements are very broad, like that of Pfizer, Inc.:

> Pfizer Inc. is a research-based global health care company. Our principal mission is to apply scientific knowledge to help people around the world enjoy longer, healthier and more productive lives. The company has four business segments: health care, consumer health care, food

science and animal health. We manufacture in 39 countries, and our products are available worldwide.

Harley-Davidson's Vision[6] is equally general:

Harley-Davidson, Inc. is an action-oriented, international company – a leader in its commitment to continuously improve the quality of mutually beneficial relationships with stakeholders (customers, dealers, employees, investors, government and society). Harley-Davidson believes the key to success is to balance stakeholders' interests through the empowerment of all employees to focus on value-added activities.

"The mission statement serves to set the organizational context within which strategic decisions will be made" is the definition we find in an article by Rebecca J. Morris.[9] This definition is very similar to the question this article is trying to answer:

What decisions should management take to define a workable Total Business Strategy which will guide functional managers in formulating their own strategy in line with the Total Business Strategy?

After reviewing a number of different mission statements, Morris finishes up with the nine components as defined by Fred R. Davis:[4]

1. *Customers:* who are the firm's customers?
2. *Product or services:* what are the firm's major products or services?
3. *Markets:* geographically, where does the firm compete?
4. *Technology:* is the firm technologically current?
5. *Concern for survival, growth, and profitability:* is the firm committed to growth and financial soundness?
6. *Philosophy:* what are the basic beliefs, values, aspirations and ethical priorities of the firm?
7. *Self-concept:* what is the firm's distinctive competence or major competitive advantage?
8. *Concern for public image:* is the firm responsive to social, community and environmental concerns?
9. *Concern for employees:* are employees a valuable asset of the firm?

This general scope of a mission statement is trying to satisfy four different groups:

1. Management – (1-4, 7).
2. Employees – (5-7, 9).
3. The community – (6, 8).
4. Shareholders – (5, 6).

But it does not give management three important features of a Total Business Strategy – attitude to risk, the decision on whether to be technology leaders or followers, and a workable definition of "concern for survival, growth and profitability".

The Missing Link – Total Business Strategy

Total Business Strategy has to answer five questions:

1. What are Our Markets?

In 1960 Theodore Levitt's article 'Marketing Myopia'[7] built a milestone in the perception of 'Business Strategy' by concluding:

In short, the organization must learn to think of itself not as producing goods or services but as *buying customers,* as doing the things that will make people *want* to do business with it.

In other words, the proper definition of "The Market Scope" is a prerequisite for success.

Since this article was published, many changes and developments have taken place in strategic thinking, but in 1995 Ron McTavish in his article 'One More Time: What Business Are You In?'[8] reminded us that:

Decisions on company scope (customer function, market segments, technology, position in value chain) are of great importance to the firm but are probably not given the attention they deserve, especially in happy economic times.

His conclusion, which is based on field research, brings back the definition of 'What are Our Markets?' to its proper place, at the heart of strategy.

In Harley-Davidson's *Operation Review* of 1996,[6] we find a declaration by Jeffrey L. Bleustein, President and Chief Operation Officer, now the Chief Executive Officer, about "the Road We're On":

Our competitors try to imitate our motorcycles, but they can't copy the intangibles that make owning a Harley-Davidson a life-fulfilling experience. We determine what's original and authentic. They're duplicating hardware, but they can only copy where we've been. They have no idea where we're going.

In this statement we can find Harley-Davidson's definition of 'What is our market?' as 'H.D. is selling 'Lifestyle Experiences' and not just motorcycles'. This definition, which is not obvious from their 'Vision' and does not appear explicitly in any strategic declaration, has directed H.D.'s actions:

- Develop a very active 'Harley Owners' Group' in the USA, in Canada, in Japan and in Europe (Germany), which is the world's largest factory-sponsored motorcycle organization, with more than 300,000 members and 900 local chapters. The HOG invites members to motorcycle shows, rallies and rides.

- Develop a large line of 'Lifestyle Products' which include clothing, footwear, electronics/prepaid calling cards, leather accessories, hats and caps, children's toys, novelties/gifts, specialties and collectibles.

- Open Harley-Davidson cafés in New York and Las Vegas.

One would have expected that with H-D's advanced technological know-how and reputation in motorcycles, they would develop a wider range of motorcycles, but they had the strategic vision to outline their market differently.

Defining the market of the firm as the needs (existing or to be developed) of its customers, is naturally the first element of Total Business strategy. It provides every one in the company with a guideline and focus as to which market is part of its strategic business and should be followed, and which is outside its normal course of business and needs strategic consideration and decision.

2. What will be our Generic Competitive Advantage?

Michael Porter defined the four 'Generic Strategies':[11, 12]

- Cost leadership
- Differentiation

- Cost focus
- Differentiation focus

Those four generic strategies, despite some of their shortcomings, have not been replaced to date and to many managers are 'The Strategy' by itself. They are the second element of Total Business Strategy.

Harley-Davidson define themselves as " ... motorcycle manufacturers and suppliers of premium quality, heavyweight motorcycles to global markets" which is the 'Differentiation Focus' type of generic competitive advantage. But, it can be regarded as only one aspect of their strategy.

3. *Are we going to be Technology Leaders or Followers?*

Technology is at the heart of almost every activity of the firm – product innovation, production, marketing, sales, customer services, etc.

A vital strategic decision should be taken by management:

In which aspect of the company activity it aims to become the 'Leader', in which a 'fast follower', and in which technology innovation decision should be taken on its own merits, without any strategic concern as to its technological state of the art.

Without such strategic decisions, a lot of efforts might be wasted to reach technological leadership in activities which do not serve the company's strategic plans, and on the other hand resources might not be directed to reach technological leadership in activities which are vital to the strategic position of the firm in its markets. Technological leadership may be 'The Competitive Advantage' or a support activity to its sustainability. Michael Porter[12] shows the relationship between competitive advantage and technological *leadership*

Technological leadership	Technological followership
Cost advantage	
• Pioneer the lowest cost product design	• Reduce the cost of the product or value creating activities by learning from the leader's experience
• Be the first firm down the learning curve	• Avoid R&D costs through imitation
• Create low-cost ways of performing value-creating activities	
Differentiation	
• Pioneer a unique product that increases buyer value	• Adapt the product or delivery system more closely to buyer needs by learning from the leader's experience
• Innovate in other activities to increase buyer value	

This decision to be 'technological leader' or 'technological follower' is the third element in Total Business Strategy.

In Harley-Davidson's *Operational Review* for 1996 we find:

> Our new Product Development Center, ... will enable us to bring new products to market faster and increase our competitive advantage.

Being a Technological Leader is considered vital to a 'Sustainable Competitive Advantage' to H-D.

4. *What is our Attitude to Risk?*

Risk is built into all aspects of the business activity. Any decision taken with a short range, long range or strategic inclination has a risk implied in choosing between alternatives-high return/high risk or low return/low risk. Yet the attitude of management to risk is hardly considered as a material part of strategy.

In *Built to Last,* Collins and Porras[2] found that "Commitment to Risk" is one more common habit of 'Visionary Companies'. Even in a most recent article "Strategy Under Uncertainty", Courtney, Kirkland and Viguerie,[3] suggest three alternatives of 'Portfolio Action', to face various levels of uncertainty in the future, namely 'No Regret Move' (low risk), 'Options' (medium risk), and 'Big Bets' (high risk), but fails to consider 'Management Attitude to Risk' as one of the influencing factors in choosing the 'Portfolio Action'.

In 1985, Richard N. Cardozo and Jerry Wind[1] concluded that: "The Monitrol" experience is not unique, and illustrates how corporate executives can use a risk-return based portfolio analysis to improve the performance of their own business. This model offers significant advantage over current 'product portfolio' approaches.

The benefit of this approach depends on the definition of the three determinants of the risk-return model:

- *The Return Hurdle Rate* – the minimum return below which the company is not interested to embark on any project even with a very low risk.
- *The Efficient Frontier* – the line which connects the points on a risk return graph, that determines the minimum return the company will accept for any project with a determined risk level.
- *The Risk Hurdle Rate* – the highest risk which is acceptable to the organization, regardless of its return.

These definitions are too crucial to the future of any company to be left to the discretion of every manager in the organization, but should be determined as part of the strategic definition.

In 1996, Harley-Davidson sold 119,000 units. They have started to build a new manufacturing plant and will have a capacity of 200,000 in 2003 – 68% increase in five years! Where should they concentrate their efforts to increase their sales? In North America, where they now have a 47% market share (down from 60.6% in 1992) and a very strong hold, and is their 'natural' market? Or target the European market, where they have only 6.8% market share and will need a lot of effort to gain a larger market share? The answer depends significantly on their 'Attitude to Risk'.

Their present attitude is conservative, as explained by Christopher Hart, a management consultant in Boston who has worked with the company and is quoted by Rifkin:[15]

> Having gone to the edge of bankruptcy twice before, Harley's top brass are in no hurry to tempt the fates again.

If they chose the 'low risk' attitude, which is their present strategy, they should go mainly to the European market in order to spread their markets and lower their exposure to the risk of unfavorable changes in the USA economy; but on the other hand, if they decide to change to 'high risk' attitude, they should go to the market which will be the easiest to enlarge – most probably the North American markets. The 'Risk Attitude' decision has a crucial strategic implication.

The risk attitude of management is the fourth element of 'Total Business Strategy'.

5. *What are our Long Range Quantitative Targets?*

Strategy is not an end in itself, but a tool to achieve the long range well-being of the company. Any strategic plan which is not accompanied by the quantitative aspect of this 'Well-Being' cannot be tested as to its feasibility, cannot be controlled nor can corrective action be taken along its implementation. Most strategic plans end up by qualitative definition, and so are the first four elements of 'Total Strategy'. But only quantitative targets, with the help of long range planning, can give us answers to questions such as:

- Are we going to achieve the long range profitability that our shareholders expect and that will insure our future as a sound and profitable business?
- Can we find, engage or build the needed resources for our strategic plans – capital, know-how, human resources, management systems, core competencies, etc.?
- Can we achieve the market share which is a major component of any strategic plan?

The quantitative targets should have at least two components:

- Market related – market share or sales growth rate,
- Result oriented – net profit, ROI, RONA, profit margin on sales, etc.

In Harley-Davidson's 'Company Status', we can find those two components:

- "Grow and maintain demand for 200,000 motorcycles unit sales by 2003 ... "
- "Drive financial results to the levels achieved by acknowledged high-performing companies."

Quantitative Targets is the fifth element of 'Total Business Strategy'.

Interdependencies

The five components of 'Total Business Strategy' are not independent decisions: Porter's view'[12] of the relations between 'Generic Competitive Advantage' and 'Technological Leadership' has been quoted earlier. Accepting high risk is a prerequisite to adopt 'Technological Leadership' of products. The 'Resource Based Attitude' relates the definition of 'What is our market?' to 'Core Competencies', which is the base of competitive advantage. Aiming at high profits (as one of the 'Quantitative Targets') must come with an acceptance of high risk. Defining a higher market share in an existing market as a 'Quantitative Target', which usually means aggressive marketing, also has to be accompanied by acceptance of higher risk. Every definition of 'Total Business Strategy' should be tested in relation to the coherence of its five components.

'Total Business Strategy' in Action

When we collect managers' statements, published information and official declarations of Harley-Davidson we find:

- *Vision.* "Harley-Davidson Inc. is an action-oriented, international company – a leader in its commitment to continuously improve the quality of mutually beneficial relationships with stakeholders (customers, dealers, employees, investors, government and society). Harley-Davidson believes the key to success is to balance stakeholders' interests through the empowerment of all employees to focus on value-added activities."

This statement provides neither definite strategy nor direction for functional managers. On the other hand, here is the company's 'Total Business Strategy':

- *What is our market?* 'Lifestyle Experiences' for heavyweight motorcycle's riders.
- *Our competitive advantage.* We will differentiate ourselves as motorcycle manufacturers and suppliers of premium quality, heavyweight motorcycles to the global markets.
- *Technological leadership.* We will be the world technological leader of the motorcycles we develop and manufacture.
- *Our attitude to risk.* Conservative.
- *Our long-range quantitative targets.* Grow and maintain the demand for 200,000 motorcycles unit sales by 2003; drive financial results to the levels achieved by acknowledged high-performing companies.

This 'Total Business Strategy' provides a complete set of strategic guidelines to formulate well coordinated 'Functional Strategies': it will give the sales manager guidelines how to make his pricing policy – high prices for differentiated products; his product policy – only products and services that strengthen the 'Harley-Davidson Life Style Experience'; his target markets – high priority to the European market, to lower the risk of dependency on the USA market, while achieving fast growth; and his promotion policy – to be directed on one hand to the present owners to upgrade their motorcycles, and on the other hand to the very well defined potential future customer – owners of competitive brands, and not-yet-owners of motorcycles which match Harley-Davidson's 'Life Style' character.

The 'Total Business Strategy' directs the operational manager as to his future production capacity – 200,000 units by 2003; and the R&D manager as to future development attitude – move forward cautiously (to lower risk) with technological improvements of present products, and the development of advanced styling to the H-D spirit. It also gives the financial manager's a 'Conservative Risk Attitude' as to where to look for his capital needs, and a profit target for his budget and control systems – financial results achieved by acknowledged high-performing companies.

The five components of Harley-Davidson's 'Total Business Strategy', although it appears not to be the result of a coherent explicit strategy formulation, do have what is expected from a 'Strategy', i.e.,

> An internally consistent set of goals and policies, for all levels of management, that collectively define the company's position in the market, the creation and exploitation of its 'distinctive competencies' and the promise of survival, growth, and profitability, with an 'Action Oriented' attitude.

Conclusion

This article suggests that in order to make Strategy Formulation practical and implementable it should consist of three elements:

- *'Mission Statement'* – the most wide scope and far future definition of purpose and strategy for the various stake-holders of the firm, which should stay unchanged for many years. This element is well known and adopted by many companies.

- *'Total Business Strategy'* – a set of five top management decisions, made inside the boundaries of the 'Mission Statement', into strategic guidelines for all management levels. The 'Total Business Strategy' should be reviewed periodically and adjusted only when major change in environment or core competencies of the company enforce it. This is the new concept presented in this article, although some of its separate building blocks are used by firms as their strategy definition.

- *'Functional Strategies'* – building the strategies for all functions of the firm in line with the 'Total Business Strategy' and in conformity one with the other. Functional strategies should be reviewed every year and adjusted within the boundaries of the 'Total Business Strategy'. Most 'Functional Strategies' are formulated today on their own, without any company-wide guidelines based only on the broad ideas of the mission statement.

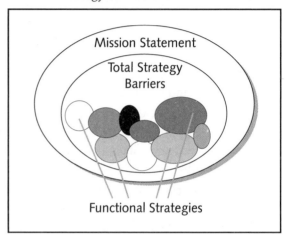

References

1. R. N. Cardozo and J. Wind, Risk Return Approach to Product Portfolio Strategy, *Long Range Planning* **18**(2), 77-85 (1985).
2. J. C. Collins and J. I. Porras, *Built to Last,* Harper Business First paperback edition, p. 220. Ibid., p. 100.
3. H. Courtney, J. Kirkland and P. Viguerie, Strategy Under Uncertainty, *Harvard Business Review* **75**(6), 67-79. (1997).
4. F. R. David, *Strategic Management* 6th edition. Prentice Hall p. 13. Ibid., p. 88. (1997).
5. G. Hamel, *European Management Journal* **11**(2), June, 152-156 (1993).
6. Harley-Davidson, Inc. All information – Company News; Letter to Shareholders; Company Status, Financial Highlights, Operation Review, H.O.G. Harley Owners' group, Lifestyle Products, have been retrieved, on December 1997, from the home page of H.D. on the Internet http://www.Harley-Davidson.com.
7. T. Levitt, Marketing Myopia, *Harvard Business Review* July/August, 45-56 (1960).
8. R. McTavish, One More Time: What Business Are You In? *Long Range Planning* **28**(2), 103-115 (1995).
9. R. J. Morris, Developing a Mission for a Diversified Company, *Long Range Planning* **28**(2), 49-60 (1996).
10. P. Pekar, Jr and S. Abraham, Is Strategic Management Living Up to Its Promise? *Long Range Planning* **28**(5), 32-44 (1995).
11. M. E. Porter, *Competitive Strategy* The Free Press, p. 35. (1980).
12. M. E. Porter, *Competitive Advantage* The Free Press, p. 20. (1985), Ibid., p. 181.
13. M. E. Porter, Towards a Dynamic Theory of Strategy, *Strategy Management Journal* **12**, 95-117 (1991).
14. M. E. Porter, What is Strategy? *Harvard Business Review* **74**(6), 61-78 (1996).
15. G. Rifkin, How Harley-Davidson Revs Its Brand, *Strategy & Business* – Booz-Allen & Hamilton, Issue 9, pp. 31-40. 4th Quarter (1997).

Strategy Implementation and Leadership

Transformational Leadership

Russell L. Ackoff

Russell Ackoff is chairman of Philadelphia-based INTERACT, the Institute for Interactive Management. One of his most recent books is *The Democratic Corporation* (Oxford University Press, 1994).

Source: *Strategy & Leadership,* Jan-Feb 1999 v27 i1 p20(6)

The large and growing literature dealing with leadership has not led to an obvious increase in either the quantity or quality of leaders, particularly transformational leaders. My cursory review of the related literature leads me to the conclusion that this lack is due to the ambiguity of the concepts of leadership and transformation.

In the minds of many people today, the terms "administration," "management," and "leadership" are interchangeable. Understanding the differences can directly improve leadership and help bring about significant organizational transformation.

- Administration consists of directing others in carrying out the will of a third party using means selected by that party.
- Management consists of directing others in the pursuit of ends and by the use of means, both of which have been selected by the manager. (Executives are managers who manage other managers.)
- Leadership consists of guiding, encouraging, and facilitating others in the pursuit of ends by the use of means, both of which they have either selected or approved.

In this formulation, leadership requires an ability to bring the will of followers into consonance with that of the leader so they follow him or her voluntarily, with enthusiasm and dedication – requirements not necessarily involved in either management or administration.

Leadership as an Aesthetic Function

Leadership has been poorly understood largely because it is primarily an aesthetic function – a concept that is also poorly understood. According to ancient Greek philosophers, continuous development depends upon the pursuit of truth, plenty, the good, and beauty/fun – aesthetics.

- The pursuit of truth is the societal function of science.
- The pursuit of plenty is a function of institutions that are concerned with (1) producing and distributing the resources that make possible the pursuit of ends as efficiently

as possible and (2) protecting the resources acquired against their appropriation, theft, or destruction.

- The pursuit of the good involves the dissemination of ethical and moral principles.
- The pursuits of beauty and fun are inseparable aspects of aesthetics. Together they make possible the continuous pursuit of ideals – ends that can be approached indefinitely but never attained.

The role of aesthetics is not well understood in our culture. Aesthetics expressed as art inspires – produces an unwillingness to settle for what we have and a desire for something better. It is both the producer and product of creative activity – change; it is essential for continuous development. Art also entertains and recreates, yielding fun in what we do, regardless of why we do it. It is the satisfaction we derive from "going there" in contrast to the satisfaction derived from "getting there." Recreation provides "the pause that refreshes." It recreates creators. We would not be able to maintain continuous pursuit of ideals without payoffs along the way. But how does all this relate to leadership?

Leadership, Vision, and Strategy

According to Jan Carlzon, the transformational leader of SAS Airlines, a leader must encourage and facilitate formulation of an organizational vision in which as many stakeholders as possible have participated. The leader must create

> an environment in which employees can accept and execute their responsibilities with confidence and finesse. He must communicate with his employees, imparting the company's vision and listening to what they need to make that vision a reality. To succeed ... he must be a visionary, a strategist, an informer, a teacher, and an inspirer.[1]

My concept of a vision is a description of a state that is considered to be significantly more desirable than the current state. It is a state that cannot be approached without a fundamental change of direction, a change of the status quo. It takes courage to lead such a change, and it requires instilling courage in others. Doing this involves more than persuasion; it requires the ability to inspire. Unlike persuasion, inspiration evokes a willingness to make sacrifices in the pursuit of long-run objectives or ideals. Therefore, visions that induce others to pursue them must be inspiring – the product of a creative act, of design. Inspiring visions are works of art, formulated by artists.

Leadership requires the ability to implement pursuit of the vision.

Inspiration without implementation is provocation, not leadership. Implementation without inspiration is management or administration, not leadership. Therefore, leaders must be both creative – in order to inspire – and courageous – in order to induce implementation.

An inspiring, courage-evoking vision requires a mobilizing idea – an idea that need not appear to be realizable. Philosopher Jose Ortega y Gasset wrote:

> [M]an has been able to grow enthusiastic over his vision of ... unconvincing enterprises. He had put himself to work for the sake of an idea, seeking by magnificent exertions to arrive at the incredible. And in the end, he has arrived there.[2]

Visions may consist of either positive or negative images. Positive images incorporate something that we do not have but want, for example, law and order, a clean, healthy environment, and peace. Negative images incorporate something that we have but do not want, for example, crime, poverty, and disease.

Negative images are much easier to formulate and to mobilize people around. However, action against negative images often results in outcomes that are less desirable than the original problem. For example, when the United States tried to get rid of alcoholism by prohibition, it got rid of neither alcoholism nor alcohol, and got organized crime. We try to get rid of crime by incarcerating criminals, despite the fact that those who have been released from prison have a higher probability of committing another, more serious crime than the one that put them in prison.

Visions as Idealized Designs

Positive visions that can mobilize transformations of individuals, organizations, or societies can be produced by idealized design. In this process those who formulate the vision begin by assuming that the system being redesigned has been completely destroyed overnight, but its environment remains exactly as it was. Then, they try to design the system that would replace the existing system right now, if they were free to replace it with any system they wanted.

The rationale for this process lies in the answers to two questions. First, if you don't know what you would do if you could do whatever you want without constraint, how could you possibly know what to do when there are constraints? Second, if you don't know what you want right now, how could you possibly know what you would want in the future?

An idealized redesign is subject to two constraints – technological feasibility and operational viability. Technological feasibility means that the design incorporates only the technology known to be feasible. This constraint is intended to prevent the design from becoming a work of science fiction. Operational viability means that the system should be designed so as to be capable of surviving in the current environment if it came into existence, but it need not be capable of doing so.

An idealized design must also be able to learn and adapt rapidly and effectively. Its product is not an ideal system because it is subject to continuous improvement. The design produced is the best ideal-seeking system that its designers can currently conceive. (They should be able to conceive of a better one in the future, however, by realizing the design objective of rapid and effective learning.)

A transformational leader, therefore, is one who can formulate or facilitate the formulation of an inspiring vision of something to be sought even if it is unattainable, although it must at least be approachable without limit. The leader must also be able to encourage and facilitate (inspire) pursuit of the vision by invoking the courage required to do so, even when short-term sacrifices are required, and by making that pursuit satisfying – fun as well as fulfilling.

Leadership Cannot Be Taught

Because leadership is essentially an aesthetic activity, it can't be taught. The most schools can do is provide some of the tools and techniques that can be used in creative work, but they cannot create creativity. One can be taught to draw, sculpt, compose, and write better than one would otherwise, but one cannot be taught to do so with creative excellence.

Students are taught to seek solutions that their teachers expect; student success depends on it. This even carries over to corporate managers who, when presented with a problem, want to know what kind of solution their bosses expect. This approach precludes creativity because creativity is the production of solutions that are not expected. Transformational leaders are driven by ideas, not by the expectations of others. They are skillful at beating the system, not surrendering to it.

Understanding Systems

A transformational leader must understand the nature of a system (including organizational systems such as a corporation, a school, a hospital, a church, or a government) and how transformation of a system differs from a transition. My definition is:

A system is a whole defined by one or more functions, and consists of two or more essential parts that satisfy the following conditions: (1) each of the parts can affect the behavior or properties of the whole; (2) none of the parts has an independent effect on the whole; the way an essential part affects the whole depends on what other parts are doing; and (3) every possible subset of the essential parts can affect the behavior or properties of the whole, but none can do so independently of the others.

Therefore, a system is a functioning whole that cannot be divided into independent parts and remain effective.

Classifying Systems

There are obviously different ways of classifying systems, depending on their intended use. For my purpose here – making clear what transformation of a system is – the critical classifying variable is purpose, and purpose is a matter of choice. An entity is purposeful if:

- It can produce the same functionally defined outcome in different ways in the same environment, for example, a person who can reach a destination by driving, using public transportation, or walking.
- It can produce functionally different outcomes in the same and different environments, for example, a person who can read in different environments and can write or converse in any of the environments in which he or she can read.

Exhibit 1 – Types of Systems

TYPE OF SYSTEM	PARTS	WHOLE
Deterministic	Not Purposeful	Not Purposeful
Animated	Not Purposeful	Purposeful
Social	Purposeful	Purposeful
Ecological	Purposeful	Not Purposeful

Although the ability to make choices is necessary for purposefulness, it is not sufficient. An entity that can behave differently but produce only one outcome in any one environment is goal-seeking, not purposeful. Control mechanisms – for example, a thermostat – are goal-seeking. In contrast, people and certain types of social groups are obviously purposeful systems.

Types of Systems

There are four basic types of systems as shown in *Exhibit 1*. These four types form a hierarchy. Animated systems have deterministic systems as their parts – various human organs operate as mechanisms. In addition, animated systems such as people can create and use deterministic systems such as clocks and automobiles, but the reverse is not true. Social systems have animated systems (people) as their parts. All three types of systems are contained in ecological systems, some of whose parts are purposeful but not the whole. For example, Earth is an ecological system that has no purpose of its own but contains social, animated, and deterministic systems.

The Business Enterprise as a System

A Deterministic System

Business enterprises were initially thought of as deterministic systems – machines created by their gods, the owners, to do their work. Enterprises, like all machines, were viewed as having no purpose of their own – only the function of serving their owners' purposes. The owners' principal purpose was to obtain an adequate return on their investment of time, money, and effort, requiring enterprises to make a profit. Making a profit was the only legitimate function of an enterprise, a belief still held by many as reflected in the writing of Milton Friedman:

> [T]here is one and only one social responsibility of business – to use its resources and engage in activities designed to increase its profits so long as it stays within the rules of the game ...[3]

Owners of early enterprises had the power to run their businesses with virtually no constraints. Although employees were recognized as human, their personal interests and purposes were irrelevant to their employers. Workers were retained only as long as they were ready, willing, and able to do what the owners wanted; then they were discarded and replaced, like replaceable machine parts, by others who were compliant and usable.

An Animated System

By the end of World War I, the mechanistic conception was largely replaced by one that was biological, organismic. People began to think about businesses as animated systems. There were a number of reasons for this transformation.

The levels of worker education and aspiration had increased largely as a consequence of compulsory public education. Government began to regulate working conditions, thereby reducing the power of the owners and protecting at least the health and safety of members of the workforce. Unions emerged, improving the conditions of work, the work itself, compensation for it, and job security. All this made the owners less god-like.

However, the most important reason for the transformation was that, even by reinvesting all their profits in growth, owners could not exploit all the growth opportunities. In addition, the increased technology of production required increased amounts of investment in facilities and equipment. Therefore, to unleash growth and productivity, many owners had to raise additional capital by selling stock, requiring most of them to relinquish at least some control over the enterprises they had created. The survival and growth rates of the enterprises that raised investment capital by "going public" were much greater than of those whose owners elected to retain control and constrain growth.

When an enterprise went public, its god disappeared. Stockholders were numerous, dispersed, anonymous, and unreachable by members of the workforce. Some of the larger corporations acquired more than a million shareholders. The principal effect of the dispersion of "ownership" was that managers gained effective control of enterprises. James Burnham referred to this as a "managerial revolution."[4] He argued that enterprises were now run by managers primarily for their own benefit, not that of the owners. Profit was considered a means, not an end. Like oxygen for a human being, profit was necessary for the survival and growth of the enterprise – not the reason for it.

Like all biological entities, the purpose of the enterprise was survival. Growth was essential. The opposite of growth – contraction – was slow death. Publicly owned enterprises were called "corporations" – derived from the Latin word "corpus," meaning "body." Moreover, in the eyes of the law, the corporation was endowed with the status of a biological individual. In 1886, the Supreme Court ruled for the first time that a corporation should be construed as a person. Biological metaphors invaded organizational thinking: the chief executive became "the head" of the organization.

Because of continuing advances in mechanization, the skills required of workers continued to increase. Those who had the required skills were not as plentiful as those who didn't. It was costly to replace skilled workers; expensive training was frequently involved. As a result, they were treated more like difficult-to-replace organs than easily replaceable machine parts. Employee health and safety received increasing attention from both unions and government. However relevant were the functions of workers in their jobs, their personal interests and purposes were not deemed an appropriate concern of their employers.

Although the biological view of the enterprise still prevails, it has eroded significantly since World War II. At that time, a major portion of the workforce was drafted into military service, and young people, the elderly, and women went to work. These replacements were motivated more by patriotism than by the need for money, as many were supported by government allowances given to dependents of servicemen. Managers who wanted high productivity could not obtain it by treating these workers as replaceable machine parts, or even as functioning organs; they had to be treated as human beings with purposes of their own. Even managers had to be treated differently because they began to behave differently. As E. E. Jennings observed:

> Then came World War II ... and innovation was needed at all levels; no one person could possibly know enough to maintain corporate viability. Corporations began placing their chips on young men not yet mesmerized by the loyalty ethic ... Young executives grew self-confident that they could manage their own careers ... When they saw upward mobility arrested, they opted for opportunities elsewhere ... The most mobile had the best chance to achieve and acquire experience; mobility bred competency that in turn bred mobility. Rapid executive turnover became a fact of life.[6]

Ex-GIs returning to civilian work wanted to be treated as unique individuals with needs and desires of their own. This was reflected in the permissive way they raised their children. As a result, the "baby boomers" of post-World War II were even less inclined than their parents to tolerate authoritarian management. They did not adopt the Protestant work ethic, and they did not consider work to be an inherently good thing. Rather they thought of work as a necessary evil or a means to an end.

Workers of the permissive generation expected their interests to be taken into account by their employing organizations. Many managers failed to do so, and alienation from work became widespread. According to a report submitted to the Secretary of Health, Education, and Welfare in 1973:

> [S]ignificant numbers of American workers are dissatisfied with the quality of their working lives. Dull, repetitive, seemingly meaningless tasks, offering little challenge or autonomy, are causing discontent among workers at all occupational levels. This is not so much because work itself has greatly changed; indeed, one of the main problems is that work has not changed fast enough to

keep up with the widespread changes in worker attitudes, aspirations, and values. A general increase in their educational and economic status has placed many American workers in a position where having an interesting job is now as important as a job that pays well. Pay is still important: it must support an "adequate" standard of living and be perceived as equitable – but high pay alone will not lead to job (or life) satisfaction.[7]

Protest groups proliferated. Consumerists and environmentalists felt they were being adversely affected by organizations of which they were not a part. These groups held corporations responsible for their allegedly harmful effects on society, its members, and the environment. This contributed to the next transformation: people began to think of the enterprise as a social system.

A Social System

Because of internally and externally applied pressures, corporate managers became aware of the need to take into account the concerns, interests, and objectives of (1) the people who were part of the systems they managed and (2) the larger systems that contained them – for example, society, and other systems and individuals who were parts of the same containing systems. In addition, these managers obviously had to be concerned with (3) the purposes of the organizations they managed.

This preoccupation with the purposes of parts and containing wholes made it increasingly difficult for managers to think of their organizations as either mechanical or biological systems. They began to think of them as systems in which people individually and collectively played the major roles.

This social, systemic view maintains that executives have duties beyond maximizing value for shareholders. For example, Hicks B. Waldron, chairman of Avon Products Inc., wrote:

> We have 40,000 employees and 1.3 million representatives around the world ... We have a number of suppliers, institutions, customers, communities. None of them have the same democratic freedom as shareholders do to buy or sell their shares. They have much deeper and much more important stakes in our company than our shareholders.[8]

A Systemic Transformation

A system is transformed when the type of system it is thought to be is changed, for example, from a deterministic or animated system to a social system responsible for the ecological systems that contain it. Therefore, a transformational leader is one who can produce or encourage and facilitate the production of a mobilizing vision of a transformed system. Equally important, the leader must be able to inspire and organize an effective pursuit of that vision and maintain it even when sacrifices are required.

The transformation of a corporation to a social system requires a number of fundamental changes:

- The traditional notion of supervision must be altered, because most employees in corporations today can do their jobs better than their bosses can. Instead, their bosses have a responsibility for creating working conditions under which their subordinates function to the best of their abilities. This requires that their subordinates have a great deal more freedom than they previously had.

- Leaders have an obligation to enable their subordinates to better themselves; that is, to provide them with opportunities for continuous development through on- and off-the-job education and training.

- Managers should manage the interactions (not the actions) of their subordinates and units with other internal and external units in order to maximize their contributions to the whole organization.

- Internal units that supply products or provide services to other internal units must be as efficient and responsive as possible to those they serve. This can be done only through competition with external sources of supply or service; that is, to operate within an internal market economy. This precludes both internal bureaucratic monopolies and the need for benchmarking. It also eliminates the generation of "make work" and the excess personnel associated with it which has led to downsizing.

- The organization's structure should be ready, willing, and able to change rapidly and effectively. Traditional tree-like hierarchies cannot do this. Several alternatives that come closer to providing the flexibility required include networks, and horizontal, matrix, and multidimensional organizations.

- The organization must be capable of rapid learning and adaptation. All learning derives from experience – our own and that of others. Mistakes are the ultimate source of learning when they are identified, diagnosed and corrected. Facilitation of these processes requires a learning-adaptation support system, one that identifies early errors in expectations, assumptions, and predictions and corrects strategies, tactics, and operations appropriately. Learning effectively from others requires a culture in which constructive conversation and discussion are continuous.

The first three requirements are best met in a democratic corporation, one in which all stakeholders can participate directly or indirectly (through elected representatives) in making decisions that affect them, and in which all with authority over others are individually subject to their collective authority.[9] Without the support of his/her subordinates, peers, and superiors, no one can manage effectively.

The transformation of a corporation from an animated system to a social system is only one kind of transformation. However, it is an essential transformation if an enterprise is to be successful in the current environment which is characterized by an increasing rate of change, interdependence, complexity, production, and dependence on knowledge and information. Only by transforming their thinking about the business enterprise will business leaders be able to achieve the necessary, focus on employees, customers, and other corporate stakeholders. A corporation that fails to see itself as an instrument of all its stakeholders will probably fail to survive in the new environment.

References

1. Jan Carlzon, *Moments of Truth* (Cambridge, Mass.: Ballinger Publishing Co., 1987).
2. Jose Ortega y Gasset, Mission of the University (New York: W. W. Norton & Co., 1956).
3. Milton J. Friedman, "The Social Responsibility of Business Is to Increase Its Profits," *The New York Times Magazine*, September 13, 1970.
4. James Burnham, *The Managerial Revolution* (New York: The John Day Co., 1941).
5. N. O. Mouzelis, "Bureaucracy," *The New Encyclopedia Britannica,* 15th Edition, Macropaedia, Vol. 3, 1974.
6. E. E. Jennings, "The World of the Executive," TWA Ambassador, 1971.
7. Work in America: Report of a Special Task Force to the Secretary of Health, Education, and Welfare (Cambridge, Mass.: The MIT Press, 1973).
8. John Hoerr and Harris Collingwood, "The Battle for Corporate Control," *Business Week,* May 18, 1987.
9. Russell L. Ackoff, *The Democratic Corporation* (New York: Oxford University Press, 1994).

Leadership
as Vision

Tony Morden

School of Business and Management, University of Teesside, Middlesbrough, UK

Source: *Management Decision* 35/9, 1997, pp. 668-676

Introduction

This article contends that leadership is a visionary concept. It analyses leadership in terms of vision. Vision is holistic; and is defined as an imagined or perceived pattern of communal possibilities to which others can be drawn, which they will wish to share, and which will constitute a powerful source of energy and direction within the enterprise.

Vision and holism

Hampden-Turner and Trompenaars (1994) comment on the holistic character of French attitudes towards issues of organization and management. The French describe such concepts as:

- *solidarisme* (mutual responsibility and interdependence);
- *1'élan vital* (the vital impulse, energizing source, or driving force);
- vision;

as key motivations for any organized community.

Mary Parker Follett (1987) describes leadership in holistic terms when she states that it is the leader who "can organize the experience of the group ... it is by organizing experience that we transform experience into power. The task of the chief executive is to articulate the integrated unity which his business aims to be ... the ablest administrators do not merely draw logical conclusions from the array of facts ... they have a vision of the future" (quoted in Hampden-Turner and Trompenaars, 1994, pp. 341-2).

Hampden-Turner and Trompenaars (1994) suggest that vision comes most easily to the holistically operating mind, while those with an analysing bias admit, like ex-President Bush of the USA, to not being "good at the vision thing".

Vision can be defined as an organized perception or phenomenon. It is an imagined or perceived pattern of communal possibilities to which others can be drawn, given the necessary enthusiasm and momentum on the part of the leader who is promulgating that vision.

Bennis (Bennis and Nanus, 1985) defines leadership in terms of the capacity to create a compelling vision, to translate it into action, and to sustain it. Bennis's 1985 study of 90 successful US public figures identified the following leadership skills:

- The ability to create a vision that others can believe in and adopt as their own. Such vision is long term in its orientation (while market imperatives are short term). The leader uses vision to build a bridge from the present to the future of the organization.
- The capacity to communicate that vision (for instance through the process of management by wandering around or MBWA described in the first of these two linked articles), and to translate it into practicalities. Its implementation, for example, might be based on the enterprise mission statement; the organization's culture and values; its mechanisms of socialization, training and development; or its systems of incentive, status and reward.
- The ability to create a climate of organizational trust. Trust acts as an emotional glue that unites leaders and followers in a common purpose, and helps achieve the outcomes of that vision. The issue of trust is dealt with in a later section of this article.

Tichy and Sherman's analysis

Tichy and Sherman (1994) first published their bestselling account of the US General Electric (GE) corporation in 1993. This in-depth and influential work describes the transformation of GE under its CEO, Jack Welch, and sparked a major renewal of academic and practitioner interest in corporate leadership. The following section of this article is based upon direct quotations from Tichy and Sherman (1994) and from Jack Welch.

Jack Welch and leadership

"Managing doesn't interest Welch much. Leadership is what he values, because that's what enhances his control over the organization" (Tichy and Sherman, 1994, pp. 195-6). "Welch's six rules:

1. control your destiny, or someone else will
2. face reality as it is, not as it was or as you wish it were
3. be candid with everyone
4. don't manage, lead
5. change before you have to
6. if you don't have a competitive advantage, don't compete". (Tichy and Sherman, 1994, p. 15)

"You don't get anywhere if you keep changing your ideas. The only way to change people's minds is with consistency. Once you get the ideas, you keep refining and improving them; the more simply your idea is defined, the better it is. And you keep communicating. Consistency, simplicity and repetition is what it's all about" (Tichy and Sherman, 1994, pp. 255-6).

Vision and leadership

"Somehow the leader and the led have to define a vision that everyone can share" (Tichy and Sherman, 1994, p. 181).

"A company should define its vision and destiny in broad but clear terms" (Tichy and Sherman, 1994, p. 298).

"Look at Winston Churchill and Franklin Roosevelt: they said, This is what it's going to be. And then they did it. Big, bold changes, forcefully articulated. When you get leaders who confuse popularity with leadership, who just nibble away at things, nothing changes" (Tichy and Sherman, 1994, p. 298).

"In the new culture, the role of a leader is to express a vision, get buy-in, and implement it. That calls for open, caring relations with employees, and face-to-face communication. People who cannot convincingly articulate a vision won't be successful" (Tichy and Sherman, 1994, p. 248).

Vision and emotional energy

"In the years ahead, corporations will sort themselves out into those that can compete on the playing field of global business, and those that either sell out or fail. Winning will require the kind of skill, speed, and dexterity that can only come from an emotionally energised work force". Bureaucratic corporations instead respond sluggishly to environmental changes. "Businesses organized on the old scientific model still build their best ideas into systems instead of encouraging employees to think for themselves. You can recognize such companies by the listlessness of their workers, who lack the conviction, spirit, and drive that characterizes champions in any field of endeavour" (Tichy and Sherman, 1994, p.13).

"The old managerial habit of imposing ideas on employees transforms concepts into rules, stripping them of their vitality. Workers change their behaviour but not their minds" (Tichy and Sherman, 1994, p. 73).

"The world of the 1990s and beyond will not belong to 'managers' or those who can make the numbers dance. The world will belong to passionate, driven leaders – people who not only have enormous amounts of energy but who can energise those whom they lead" (Tichy and Sherman, 1994, p. 182).

"Executives have substantial power over employees, but they can't tell people what to believe. Creating the pumped-up, turned-on workforce that Welch envisions requires an honest intellectual exchange between bosses and subordinates – conducted as a dialogue of equals. Welch calls this 'leading while being led'" (Tichy and Sherman, 1994, p. 75).

"One of Welch's main goals as a manager has been to stimulate positive emotional energy in subordinates. He says he wants 'turned on people'" (Tichy and Sherman, 1994, p. 62).

The values represented by the vision

"The goal was to implant and nourish the values Welch cherishes: self-confidence, candour, and an unflinching willingness to face reality even when it's painful" (Tichy and Sherman, 1994, p. 4).

"The new organization at GE ... depends on shared values ... the values-based organization ... derives its efficiency from consensus: workers who share their employer's goals don't need much supervision" (Tichy and Sherman, 1994, p. 4).

"The most effective competitors in the twenty-first century will be the organizations that learn how to use shared values to harness the emotional energy of employees. As speed, quality and productivity become more important, corporations need people who can instinctively act the right way without instructions, and who feel inspired to share their best ideas with their employers. That calls for emotional commitment. You can't get it by pointing a gun. You can't buy it, no matter how much you pay. You've got to earn it, by standing for values that other people want to believe", want to identify with, "and by consistently acting on those values" (Tichy and Sherman, 1994, p. 195).

Welch "pushes values because that's the way to get results. Delegating more of the control function to individuals ... reduces the need for reports, reviews, and other external mechanisms. A boundaryless organization can achieve the same level of control as a hierarchical one – but at less cost, with less friction, and faster" (Tichy and Sherman, 1994, p. 195).

Architecture and trust

Bennis and Townsend (1995) suggest that a key to competitive advantage in the years to come will be the visionary capacity of leaders to create a social architecture that is capable of generating intellectual and social capital, and capable of adding value. This capital will be manifest in the value addition that results from the generation of ideas, knowledge, expertise, and innovation. Such social architecture is likely to be based on high levels of trust.

Architecture

Kay (1993) identifies four sources (or "foundations") of corporate success. These are:
1. architecture;
2. innovation (which may be imitated), and additionally an architecture that is capable of sustaining a process of ongoing innovation (which may be much more difficult, or even impossible for competitors to imitate);
3. brands and corporate reputation;
4. the possession of, or access to some key strategic asset.

Kay suggests that the key measure of corporate success is that of added value. Added value is the difference between the value of outputs and the relative cost of the inputs required to create them. Kay contends that the purpose of enterprise activity is to put together a set of relationships (architecture), to innovate, to develop the long-term value of brands and reputation, and to seek strategic assets such that the generation of added value is achieved within the prevailing conditions.

The enterprise is defined by its contracts and relationships. Added value is created by the success in putting together these contracts and relationships, so it is the quality and distinctiveness that enterprise leadership can bring to these contracts and relationships that determine the amount of value addition (and hence the degree of corporate success).

Architecture is defined by Kay as the network of relational contracts (defined below) within and around the enterprise. Organizations may establish these relationships with and among their employees (internal architecture); with their customers and suppliers (external architecture); and among groups of institutions engaged in related activities (networks; partnerships; value adding partnerships; holonic networks and virtual companies [which are defined as configurations of independent organizations that act in an integrated manner to meet emerging business opportunities]; etc).

The value-adding potential of enterprise architecture will derive from the relative success of those who establish it to create and sustain organizational knowledge and competence; to create and sustain experience; to achieve flexible and ongoing responses to changing circumstances; to create open and useful exchanges of information; and to create internalized cultural disciplines of motivation, quality and control.

A key part of Kay's analysis is that architecture and social capital can only be created, sustained, and protected from imitation if it is contained within a framework of relational contracts. What can be written down in a standard or classical contract can be reproduced. Architecture therefore depends:

- on the ability of enterprise leadership to build and sustain long-term relationships characterized by trust and the pursuit of mutual benefit (for instance as described elsewhere by Ouchi, 1981 as "Theory Z"); and

- on the ability of enterprise leadership to establish an environment that discourages (or makes unnecessary) "opportunistic" short-term behaviour. Opportunistic behaviour by individuals is likely by definition to be counter-productive to long-term value generation (especially where the individual has been able to appropriate some of the value they has generated to themself).

Long-term enterprise relationships must therefore be mutually profitable, for instance taking the form of the offer of "noticeably fatter paychecks" (Tichy and Sherman, 1994, p. 217), employment guarantees, or significant length-of-service based bonuses, in return for personal flexibility and commitment. They might instead take the form of long-term supply contracts framed within partnership sourcing agreements, etc).

Trust

Fukuyama (1995), like Tichy and Sherman (1994), suggests that the most effective organizations are based on communities of shared ethical values. These communities do not require extensive contractual or legal regulation of their relations and social architecture because prior moral consensus gives members of the group a basis for mutual trust. Fukuyama comments that

> social capital has major consequences for the nature of the industrial economy that society will be able to create. If people who have to work together in an enterprise trust one another because they are all operating according to a common set of ethical norms, doing business costs less. Such a society will be better able to innovate organizationally since the high degree of trust will permit a wide variety of social relationships to emerge. Hence the ... sociable Americans pioneered the development of the modern corporation ... (while) the Japanese have explored the possibilities of network organizations ... By contrast, people who do not trust one another will end up co-operating only under a system of formal rules and regulations, which have to be negotiated, agreed to, litigated, and enforced (if necessary by coercive means). This legal apparatus, serving as a substitute for trust, entails what economists call "transaction costs". Widespread distrust in a society, in other words, imposes a kind of tax on all forms of economic activity, a tax that high-trust societies do not have to pay (Fukuyama, 1995, pp. 27-8).

Fukuyama (1995) suggests that a high degree of trust increases economic efficiency by reducing these transaction costs that would otherwise be incurred, for instance in:

- maintaining and sustaining an effective enterprise relationship architecture;
- holding together large-scale and impersonal organizations or networks whose relationships must have a wider basis than that restricted to family or kin;
- dealing with inter-party disputes;
- finding trustworthy and reliable suppliers, buyers, or creditors;
- negotiating and implementing contractual arrangements;

- complying with government, trade, or environmental regulations;
- identifying, and dealing with malpractice or fraud.

Such transactional arrangements are made easier (and less expensive) if the relationship architecture is characterized by honesty. For instance, there will be:

- less need for control mechanisms within the management process;
- less need to specify matters contractually;
- there will be fewer grounds for dispute; and hence fewer disputes;
- less need for litigation (which consumes wealth but adds little or no value; destroys relationships; and reduces trust);
- less need to hedge against unexpected contingencies and unpredictable issues.

At the same time, Fukuyama (1995) contends that societies manifesting a high degree of communal solidarity and shared values may be more efficient than their more individualistic counterparts in that they may lose less value from "free riders". Free riders benefit from value generation by an organization or a society but do not contribute proportionately (or at all) to the effort by which that value is generated. The free rider problem is a classic dilemma of group behaviour.

One solution to the free rider problem involves the group imposing some sort of coercion or discipline on its members to limit the amount of free riding that they can do. This might involve the classical use of frequent and close monitoring and supervision (which is expensive; and which as a form of control may be resented by the "non free riders" in the community who are pulling their weight).

Equally, but more efficiently, the incidence of free riding could instead be mitigated if the group possesses a high degree of social solidarity. People become free riders where they put their individual interests ahead of the group. But if they strongly identify their own well-being with that of the group, or put the group's interests ahead of their own in the relative scale of priorities, they may be less likely to shirk work or avoid responsibilities. Hence, within business organizations, sensitive leaders will attempt to establish a culture of pride, equality, a sense of belonging, and a sense of *esprit de corps* among their employees such that these people believe that they are part of a worthwhile enterprise which has a valuable purpose.

The high-trust workplace

Fukuyama describes lean manufacturing, for instance as found in the automobile industry, as an example of the organization and management of a high-trust workplace. It can be contrasted with the classic low-trust manufacturing system created by F.W. Taylor and the School of Scientific Management (for instance, see Morden, 1996).

Lean manufacturing systems require a high level of trust because, for example:

- the fragility of the system, which can easily be disrupted, calls for responsible behaviour throughout the network upon which it is based, at all times. This applies equally to suppliers and employees;
- people are trusted to deal with problems, where and when they happen, at source.

This is because:

- people are trusted with high levels of responsibility and discretion at all points of the supply and operational process. This implies a significant degree of the delegation of authority and responsibility throughout the workforce and the supply chain;

- the use of collective and team/cell-based operational structures means that free-riding behaviour becomes unacceptable. Group norms become dominant (particularly if pay is also based on them) over individualistic priorities;

- the abandonment by employees of traditional lines of demarcation and trade union involvement in the establishment of work practices must be reciprocated by management. This may mean making available the necessary multi-skill and quality assurance training; providing employment guarantees (at least to core workers); implementing single employee status, and the downgrading/elimination of hierarchical privilege; increased remuneration resulting from increased productivity, etc);

- there will be an expectation of totally cooperative and trustworthy behaviour by suppliers and intermediaries throughout the value chain. This is related to the requirement that open information flows are needed to make the system work. The free exchange of information will only occur where there is adequate trust between the parties to that exchange. This is particularly true of the supply chain; and of network structures/ relationship architectures.

Collins and Porras' analysis

Collins and Porras' (1996) influential study, *Built To Last,* may be described as an inheritor of a lengthy (and US dominated) tradition of the study of corporate performance. This tradition is based on the work of such academics, consultants, and corporate leaders as Frederick Taylor, Alfred Sloane, Peter Drucker, Tom Peters, and Rosabeth Moss Kanter.

Collins and Porras (1996) suggest that their study identifies the main characteristics of what they call "visionary companies". These companies are all American, with the exception of the Sony Corporation. These companies are described as being characterized by excellence. Collins and Porras (1996) define such companies, which include 3M, Hewlett-Packard, Johnson and Johnson, and Boeing, as "premier institutions – the crown jewels – in their industries, widely admired by their peers and having a long track record of making a significant impact on the world around them ... visionary companies prosper over long periods of time, through multiple product life cycles and multiple generations of active leaders" (Collins and Porras, 1996, pp. 1-2).

Company sample and research methodology

Collins and Porras (1996, p. 2) note that "in a six-year research project, we set out to identify and ... research the historical development of a set of visionary companies, to examine how they differed from a carefully selected control set of comparison companies, and to thereby discover the underlying factors that account for their ... long term position".

The primary objectives for the research project were to:

1. identify the underlying characteristics common to visionary companies (that distinguish them from other companies), and to translate these findings into a useful conceptual framework;

2. communicate these concepts and findings so that they may influence the practice of management and prove beneficial to people who want to create, develop, and maintain visionary companies.

The survey was based on a sample of 18 companies, all founded before 1950. These were compared with an equivalent set of comparison companies, in order to establish what distinguishes one set of companies from another.

These sample companies were analysed in depth across their entire history. The researchers sought "underlying, timeless, fundamental principles and patterns that might apply across eras" (Collins and Porras, 1996, p. 17). This analysis was based on the study of:

> nine categories of information over the entire history of each company. These categories encompassed virtually all aspects of a corporation, including organization, business strategy, products and services, technology, management, ownership structure, culture, values, policies, and the external environment. As part of this effort, we systematically analysed annual financial statements back to the year 1915 and monthly stock returns back to the year 1926. In addition, we did an overview of general and business history in the United States from 1800 to 1900, and an overview of each industry represented by the companies in our study (Collins and Porras, 1996, p. 19).

Collins and Porras' proposition

Collins and Porras (1996) propose a model of a visionary company. This model is characterized by:

*   *Clock building, not time-telling,* by which the company itself is the ultimate creation. The builders of such companies take an architectural approach and concentrate on developing the key organizational traits of the visionary company. Building a vision and a company that can prosper far beyond the presence of any single leader and through multiple life cycles is described as "clock building".

*   *More than profits.* The visionary company is driven by a powerful internal core ideology which comprises core values and a sense of purpose which extend far beyond simply making money. This "pragmatic idealism" guides and inspires people, and remains relatively fixed for long periods of time. The core ideology is seen as a primary element in the historical development and success of the visionary company

*   *Preserve the core but stimulate progress.* The visionary company protects and preserves its core ideology but puts in place a relentless drive for progress that implies development and change in all of the activities inspired by that core ideology. Visionary companies are characterized by strong drives for exploration and discovery for creativity and innovation, for improvement, and for change.

*   *Big hairy audacious goals (or BHAGs).* Visionary companies will deliberately set themselves audacious and risky objectives, some of which will "bet the company" (Deal and Kennedy 1988). Such objectives (for example the development of the Boeing 747) will challenge the whole company and force change upon it, as well as reinforcing the market leadership typically enjoyed by these premier companies.

*   *Cult-like cultures.* The company's core ideology is translated into clear cultural and behavioural patterns. These cultural and ideological patterns are imposed on people in the organization, who are screened and indoctrinated into conformity and commitment to them. There are high levels of expected commitment; those who cannot

accept the prevailing culture will leave or be fired. Visionary companies tend to be more demanding of their employees and managers than other companies. But those who can cope may develop a strong sense of working for an elite organization, which in turn has an effect on the calibre of people who can be attracted and recruited. Visionary companies may be regarded as ultimate employers who are in a position to recruit "the best".

- *Try a lot of stuff and keep what works.* Visionary companies exhibit high levels of action and experimentation – often unplanned or undirected – that produce new or unexpected paths of progress. This evolutionary progress is opportunistic in character; accepts the value of trial-and-error and chance discovery; and rejects 'Not Invented Here' limitations on the strategic management of technology and innovation. Individual employees are encouraged and empowered to seek new paths and new ways of doing things.

- *Home-grown management.* Visionary companies select, develop, and promote managerial talent from inside the company to a greater degree than other organizations. This brings to senior levels only those who have spent considerable time being socialized into, and internalizing the core ideology of the company. This has the effect of preserving and reinforcing the core ideology, and bringing about continuity. For instance, in commenting on the track record and succession planning of the US General Electric corporation (GE), Collins and Porras (1996, p. 171) comment that "to have a Welch-calibre CEO is impressive. To have a century of Welch-calibre CEOs all grown from inside ... that is one key reason why GE is a visionary company".

- *Good enough never is.* The visionary companies are characterized by an ethic of continuous self-improvement, with the aim of doing better and better in the future. This helps to stimulate progress. The search for improvement becomes a way of life – a habit of mind and action. Collins and Porras (1996) suggest that excellent performance comes naturally to the visionary company as a result of a never-ending cycle of self-stimulated improvement and investment for the future. One consequence of this ethic is that visionary companies tend to install powerful mechanisms to create discomfort and to obliterate complacency As a result, such companies may not be "comfortable" places in which to work!

Mind of a manager, soul of a leader

Hickman's (1992) influential study *Mind of a Manager, Soul of a Leader* was first published in 1990. Hickman compares and inter-relates the competencies and mind-sets of managers and those of leaders. He notes that as a result of the growing pressures on contemporary organizations, "executives find themselves confronted with an escalating conflict between the managerial and leadership requirements of organizations. An 'either/or' mentality dominates at a time when organizations most desperately need the best of both" (pp. vii-viii). Hickman (1992) attempts to put to rest fruitless "debate about 'managers' and 'leaders' ... (suggesting that) what companies need are the skills of both; the practical, analytical, orderly mind of a manager; and the experimental, visionary, creative soul of a leader" (endpapers).

Hickman (1992, p. 7) suggests that "the words 'manager' and 'leader' are metaphors representing two opposite ends of a spectrum. 'Manager' tends to signify the more analytical, structured, controlled, deliberate, and orderly end of the continuum; while 'leader' tends to occupy the more experimental, visionary, flexible, uncontrolled, and creative end".

A fundamental holistic objective should be to blend strong management and strong leadership into one integrated whole, where the strengths of both combine synergistically and offset each other's weaknesses. This synergy might be achieved by any or all of the permutations described below.

Authority plus influence

Authority gives someone the legitimate right to order and command behaviour. Managers use authority to get people to take action. Influence involves the use of indirect or intangible means to prompt thought, opinion, attitude, and behaviour.

Leaders apply influence rather than authority to get people to take action. They are able to rally others behind the vision or purpose they have articulated.

Hickman (1992, p. 102) comments that the organization "needs leaders with strong influence and managers who use authority to get things done. Balanced attention to both allows an organization to focus on the key issues facing it, as well as on the nuts and bolts of daily operation".

Art plus science

Leaders may value the fluid, intuitive, and qualitative side of their work, thinking of it as an art. This may cause them to think and communicate in terms of visions and beliefs.

Managers will often conceptualize their work as a precise, rational, and qualitative science. Given this tendency, managers typically study, define, and attempt to clarify the concrete, measurable aspects of organization and management. Some will dismiss the concept of organizational leadership as a "soft" issue, of little worth compared with the "hard" matters of management science.

The enterprise in reality needs both approaches to be effective and responsive, even if these approaches co-exist in a state of tension.

Simplicity plus complexity

Hickman (1992) notes in this context *McNamara's First Law of Analysis,* which states that a person should "always start by looking at the grand total. Whatever problem you are studying, back off and look at it in the large". Hickman suggests that when a leader wishes to view this full picture, they may do so by simplifying it. The leader searches for patterns, connections, frameworks, or concepts that encompass all the confusing details surrounding a particular issue. As a result of this inclination, leaders tend to create simple visions or perceptions of reality, encouraging a philosophy of keep it simple (KIS). Leaders use the detail to find patterns and frameworks in order to simplify the complexity.

When looking at the same situations, managers may tend to see complexity. When attempting to conceptualize and understand the whole picture, the manager's mind may turn to the detail, digging for additional data that may not be readily apparent. Given this inclination (reinforced by the tendency of Western managers to receive analytical, deconstructionist, and problem-orientated education and training), managers may create complex analyses of reality that contain all of the detail they can muster. Managers use details to paint the most realistic picture possible, with all its complexity.

Hickman (1992, p. 163) comments that "in cases of complexity versus simplicity, it may be easier for the manager to embrace some or part of the orientation of the leader than for the leader to assume some or part of the orientation of the manager". He suggests that "organizations should look for complexity first and then find ways to simplify that complexity. Both orientations are … important, but simplicity alone carries much more risk … in an increasingly global and complex world. However, complexity in and of itself can fail because it obscures simple strategic priorities and cultural values that need to be clearly … communicated to people throughout the organization. In a balanced and integrated organization, managers work to bring the full picture with all its complexity into focus, while leaders complement their efforts by taking that complex picture and finding simple patterns and frameworks to make it easy to use and communicate" (Hickman, 1992, p. 164).

Dreams plus duties

Hickman (1992) suggests that when leaders want to enhance their effectiveness, they pursue dreams because dreams represent new visions and new possibilities. Leaders may evaluate their performance on the basis of dreams achieved.

In their drive to become effective, managers will instead focus on duties because duties represent concrete and finite tasks. Hickman suggests that when managers appraise and evaluate their performance, they instinctively use current duties as their measurement standards.

Hickman (1992) comments that both dreams and duties are needed, because both "are inexorably linked" (p. 223).

Inspiration plus instruction

Because managers want to ensure that their people know what to do and how to do it, they tend to take an instructional approach to their subordinates. Such an approach emphasizes the "how" of individual and organizational performance; and relies on training to make sure the "how" can be turned into capability.

On the other hand, leaders, wanting to make sure that their people know "why" their jobs are important, may try harder to inspire. Inspiration, as a form of motivation, is seen as the best way of helping people grasp the meaning and outcome of their work. Leaders will be well advised to ensure that people are properly instructed and trained in the "hows", but only after focusing on the "whys" and their attendant vision and inspiration.

Fasten plus unfasten

Hickman suggests that the management process tends to fasten matters in two ways:
1. managers fasten their attention on specific issues;
2. managers then attempt to fasten resolutions to those issues onto people and organization.

As a result, managers will set performance and behaviour priorities, objectives, policies, expectations, milestones, assignments and tasks that will lead towards the resolution of these matters.

Leaders tend instead to unfasten matters in two ways:
1. they will tend to focus their gaze away from immediate concerns, and visualize the larger context or wider picture;
2. they like to unfasten apparent narrowly focused or "tied-down" aspects of their people and organization.

In this way, leaders may disdain existing direction, immediate priorities, prevailing expectations, and current objectives. They may question the "received wisdom", challenging what they perceive as potentially myopic, conservative, or static views of the market, technology, competitors, culture, etc; and past organizational responses to these variables. Their objective may be to evaluate and review, to create or innovate, to challenge self-imposed "not-invented-here" restrictions, to change the parameters of the enterprise, or to achieve breakthroughs in their critical success factors.

Compromise plus polarize

A manager's mind may seek compromise, whether with superiors, peers, or subordinates, in order to ensure that policies, plans and programmes get implemented. Compromising may become a way of life for managers, for without it the organization may get enmeshed in a rising tide of conflicts and differences. Compromise is used to reduce or eliminate conflict.

The leader may instead seek to polarize. Leaders may deliberately attempt to elicit strong, diametrically opposed responses from superiors, peers, and subordinates. Polarization of viewpoints is useful because it reveals the multiplicity of perspectives that enrich an undertaking, and demonstrates alternative visions or possibilities.

Hickman (1992) contends that both compromise and polarization are needed. He comments that "there is a time for iron-willed polarizing, and there is a time for flexible compromising. If you only know how to compromise, you miss the tonic effect of polarizing; if you only know how to polarize, you miss those opportunities where ... bending could save the day" (p. 158).

Vision plus version

A prime leadership skill will be to envision some desired future state of being, and to inspire others to understand and share that vision. However, after the leader has envisioned and conceptualized that desired future state of being, someone else usually has to create a version of that desired state in order to implement it. This raises two issues:

1. the developing relationship between what was envisioned and what can be realistically implemented;
2. the leader's perception of (and satisfaction with) the process of versioning and implementation; and his/her capacity to leave the versioning of vision to others.

Hickman comments that the enterprise needs both visioning and versioning capabilities to sustain it over the long term.

Present plus future

Hickman suggests that managers' minds typically think about and act on the present. When managers do look into the future, they may do so by extrapolating from the past and present. For these managers, the present represents the boundary of their accountability. They perceive that the only way to create the future is to manage the present.

Leaders' souls, on the other hand, reside in the future, viewing the present in terms of its long-term implications. The present functions primarily as a measure of progress towards some future envisioned state. Leaders perceive their accountability to be defined in terms of future change, progress, or results.

In reality, the direction of the enterprise depends on the effective management of both present and future, not one or the other.

Short term plus long term

Managers tend to focus on short-term, immediate results. They may view such results as the key measure of whether or not they are doing a good job.

Leaders will tend to think in the long-term of wider issues and results. They believe that focusing on the long-term places the short-term in its proper perspective.

In reality both short and long-term results are important considerations for any organization. Hickman (1992) comments that "while the company should not pursue short-term results at the expense of long-term results, neither should it use the pursuit of long-term results to justify poor performance in the short-term" (p. 256).

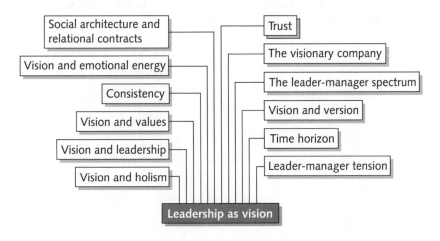

Figure 1. A model of leadership as vision

Summary

The model of leadership described in this article is illustrated in Figure 1. The diagram summarizes the key variables described in this article that comprise the model of leadership as vision. A related article, published in *Management Decision,* Vol. 35 No. 7, analysed leadership as competence.

References

1. Bennis, W. and Nanus, B. (1985), *Leaders: the Strategies for Taking Charge,* Harper & Row, New York, NY.
2. Bennis, W. and Townsend, R. (1995), *Reinventing Leadership,* Piatkus, London.
3. Collins, J. C. and Porras, J. I. (1996), *Built to Last,* Century Business, London.
4. Deal, T. E. and Kennedy, A. A. (1988), *Corporate Cultures,* Penguin, London.
5. Follett, M. P. (1987), *Freedom and Co-ordination: Lectures in Business Organization,* Garland, New York, NY.
6. Fukuyama, F. (1995), *Trust: The Social Values and the Creation of Prosperity,* Hamish Hamilton, London.
7. Hampden-Turner, C. and Trompenaars, F. (1994), *The Seven Cultures of Capitalism,* Piatkus, London.

8. Hickman, C. R. (1992), *Mind of a Manager, Soul of a Leader,* Wiley, New York, NY.
9. Kay, J. (1993), *Foundations of Corporate Success,* Oxford University Press, Oxford.
10. Morden, A. R. (1996), *Principles of Management,* McGraw-Hill, London.
11. Ouchi, W. (1981), *Theory Z,* Addison-Wesley, Reading, MA.
12. Tichy, N. M. and Sherman, S. (1994), *Control Your Own Destiny or Someone Else Will,* Harper Business, New York, NY.

Application questions

1. How well are we developing, training, schooling leaders as opposed to managers? What are or should be the main differences in developing leaders as distinct from developing managers?
2. Can a leader lead with a vision?
3. What would be the ideal characteristics of a leader in your organization in the near future? How would they spend their days at work?

A Portfolio of Strategic Leaders

William E. Rothschild

William Rothschild has led his own consulting practice in Strategic Leadership since 1984, after serving as corporate planner at General Electric. He is the author of four internationally acclaimed books on strategic thinking, management, and leadership. His latest book is *Risktaker, Caretaker, Surgeon, Undertaker: The Four Faces of Strategic Leadership*, published by John Wiley (1993).

Source: *Planning Review*, January/February 1996, pp. 16-19.

S trategic leadership is really very simple – determine where you want to invest, develop a competitive strategic advantage, and get the right leader, who will then select the right team. From there, it is just good management. Unfortunately, many companies don't link the leader with the team and the strategy. Unless all of the pieces fit together, the business will fail.

Three factors are key to successful strategic leadership:

- *Leader and life-cycle phase must be matched.* All successful companies have a portfolio of products and probably businesses. Some are growing, others maturing, and still others declining. A different type of leader is required to lead a business in each of the life-cycle phases. Each phase requires specific attitudes and skills in dealing with change and risk.

- *Each strategic differentiator requires a different leader and implementation team.* All successful business units or product lines have a strong, lasting, competitive advantage or differentiator. Some are differentiated by their ability to market and sell, some by their ability to innovate and create new products or services, and others by their ability to produce more for less. Leader and team must match the strategic driver.

- *Just as strategies must change, so must leadership.* Timing is the key – nothing lasts forever. A strategy may have been successful for a decade or more; a leader may have an unblemished track record and a string of winning years; but neither of these facts can guarantee success in the future.

Matching the Leader to the Business

One of the reasons strategic management became so popular in the 1970s and early 1980s was that many companies had grown by acquisitions and diversification. These companies found that one strategy wouldn't work in all of their different businesses. Further, they found that some of the business units or product lines were profitable and attractive to the company, while others were not. The tools of strategic thinking helped them sort out the differences and make decisions about where to focus limited resources. Strategic thinking improved their ability to restructure and spin off unwanted product lines and units, and helped them to determine what acquisitions would enhance their strengths and make them leaders in their targeted markets.

Successful companies need strong, profitable business units to provide the cash to invest in future growth opportunities. Companies that can't finance their growth tend to fail because of the burden of debt and the need to think and manage for the short term. Witness the power of Microsoft, which has an enviable portfolio of products and has been able to grow and become a market leader while staying out of debt. Strategic thinking forces a recognition of business differences and the need to have different strategies and resource allocation systems to deal with each type of business. Successful companies must have the ability to select and place the right leader in the right job at the right time.

As a corporate planner at General Electric, I was personally involved in making these assessments and decisions. GE was and is a very complex company – it is a perfect example of a "portfolio" company. We found that GE, like most large companies, had a full spectrum of winners and losers. Smaller companies also have portfolios, but they may contain an assortment of product lines rather than complete businesses.

If you accept the fact that a company may have a portfolio of businesses or products, it should be obvious that this company will need a portfolio of leaders. Have you ever seen a successful growth business led by a low-risk "micro-manager"? Have you witnessed the frustration of a high-risk-taker trying to manage a conservative, incremental business, or even worse trying to lead a business that needs to be pruned?

It happens, and it is disastrous. People have failed and business units and product lines have failed, all because they had the wrong kind of leader. The following steps can be used as a guideline for matching the leader with the needs of the company.

Step #1: Make sure the leader has the right risk profile and time horizon.

Businesses and product lines, like people, go through four basic stages. The first stage is birth and childhood; the second is early adulthood; third is maturity; and the last is old age and death. Exhibit 1 shows the cycles of a business and the type of leader required to implement the necessary strategies in each stage. Risktakers are required when a business is embryonic and in the beginning of its life cycle. Once the business reaches a certain size and magnitude, the qualities of a caretaker are required. As the company matures, pruning will be necessary and the talents of a skilled surgeon are needed. Finally a business or a product may have to be "put to rest," and an undertaker takes over. The

Exhibit 1 – Linking Strategy and Leaders

Caretaker
- builds on strengths
- creates gradual change
- willing to commit to longer term

Surgeon
- is selective
- knows what is attractive
- is decisive
- makes tough decisions
- holds nothing "sacred"

Risktaker
- is a visionary
- is aggressive
- is highly intuitive
- creates dynamic change
- has "killer" instinct

Undertaker
- selects the best
- liquidates
- is compassionate

| Birth/Childhood | Adult | Maturity | Old Age/Death |
| Embryonic | Rapid Growth | Slow Growth | Decline |

talents of each of these types of leader are very distinctive. It is rare that one individual can do it all.

The emergence of reengineering and restructuring as a business strategy indicates that it is not inevitable that companies die. The right strategic leader can re-focus the company and position it for a new cycle of sustained growth as shown in Exhibit 2. Initially reengineering and restructuring require the talents of the surgeon leader. These surgeons must refuse to hold anything sacred. They must systematically determine

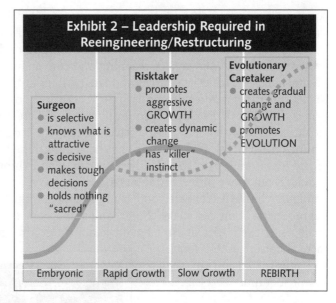

Exhibit 2 – Leadership Required in Reeingineering/Restructuring

Surgeon
- is selective
- knows what is attractive
- is decisive
- makes tough decisions
- holds nothing "sacred"

Risktaker
- promotes aggressive GROWTH
- creates dynamic change
- has "killer" instinct

Evolutionary Caretaker
- creates gradual change and GROWTH
- promotes EVOLUTION

Embryonic   Rapid Growth   Slow Growth   REBIRTH

which pieces of the company are most attractive to retain, and which are unattractive or lack a true strategic fit. There have been examples of companies whose leaders were caretakers or "premature undertakers," who tried to do the restructuring gradually while protecting the folklore and "heritage of the company." These efforts failed.

Successful surgeons, however, don't have a fire sale. They recognize that all assets have value, and they seek out companies that need or want the businesses they plan to discard. GE's Jack Welch is a master at divesting at a profit. He took RCA apart piece-by-piece, sold or traded what he didn't want, and kept what he believed would increase GE share-holder value.

The real issue is what happens after the surgery is complete. Too much surgery or an obsession with continual cost cutting results in "corporate anorexia" and a slow painful death. When the surgery is successfully implemented, the surgeon leader should step aside and be replaced with a "dynamic top-line grower," a risktaker leader. Or, if the time permits, the talents of an evolutionary caretaker may be appropriate, provided the care-taker leader focuses on continuing to grow both the top line (revenues) and the bottom line (earnings) on the income statement.

Classifying businesses or products into these stages of evolution will help you to determine whether or not current leaders fit the requirements of the business. The worst scenario is to have extremes in the jobs. Picture Bill Gates assigned to lead IBM's mainframe business. He would either go crazy, resign, or kill the business prematurely. The same is true of a surgeon leader who is assigned to run a growth business. The surgeon would focus on cutting out and reducing costs instead of investing for growth. Every time this mismatch happens, it has had negative results.

Step #2: Match the leader to the strategic differentiator.

The second step of strategic thinking and decision making is to determine how the organization can gain and maintain a sustainable competitive advantage by careful analy-sis of the current and anticipated market, the customers, the competitors, and changing industry characteristics. The key is to find a strength that can be used to beat the competitors. Some companies create a sustainable competitive barrier by focusing on *what* they sell: innovative, differentiated products and services. Others create a difference by focusing on *how* they sell: they create unique and strong sales and distribution networks or different ways of reaching and converting customers. Still others use their unique ability to make or source products perhaps at the *lowest cost* in responding rapidly to customer and market demands. Then there are companies that have used their *strong financial position* to develop a unique advantage. Of greatest importance is that the strategic differentiators are real competitive, sustainable strengths, not just desires or wishes.

Once the strategic differentiator has been determined, it is critical to match the talents of the leader and team to the differentiator. (See Exhibit 3.) Lest we forget, leaders are people. People have different talents and skills as well as different tolerances for risk and ambiguity. Some leaders are good at marketing and sales, others at creating and innovating products. Some can make things, and still others are good score keepers and financial analysts. If the leader doesn't have the ability, commitment, and motivation to implement the strategic differentiator and gain the advantage, then a new leader must be assigned to do the job.

How often have you seen a financial expert succeed in a marketing and sales-driven company? Or have you seen a marketing professional succeed in a situation that required the talents of a financial leader? In most companies, a mismatch of talents and strategic needs equals failure for the leader, the company, and even society.

Exhibit 3 – Matching Strategic Differentiators and Leader Talents	
Differentiators	**Leader Talents**
What to Sell (Products/Applications)	Product/Service innovation Problem-solving skills
How to Sell (Approaches/Distribution)	Selling/Marketing skills Relationship orientation
How to Make/Source	Production/Logistics skills Costs/Efficiency orientation
How to Finance	Financial creativity

Step #3: Match the team to the leader and the strategy.

Suppose the business unit is going to use "marketing and sales" as its strategic differentiator. It plans to outmarket and outsell its competitors, which is a typical strategy in highly aggressive and dynamic markets. This ability is clearly the differentiator in the personal computer and software markets. Bill Gates is "out-hyping" even the best of the packaged goods industry leaders. What constitutes the right team required to support a leader with this job?

- The product designers must package the product to appeal to the market. The product must look the part, and its features must be appealing and easy to use.
- The sales force must be highly aggressive and have a strong "missionary instinct." It must get prime shelf space in the stores and be unwilling to take a secondary position. Advertising must be aggressive, timely, and strongly related to the reasons the customer buys.
- The logistical system must be in place so that there are no stock-outs.
- Finally, the team must be willing to fix the customer's problem quickly. If the customer can't get Windows 95 to work, the 800 number must be highly responsive.

In short, the team must be dynamic, aggressive, and competitive, as well as flexible and creative. It must meet or exceed customer expectations. (Note: This may be the one part of the Gates strategy that will be a major problem. He has created very high expectations, which could disappoint many users.)

Now suppose the strategic differentiator of the business unit is "high volume and low cost." The team would be quite different. The organization, compensation, and reward systems would also be different. The leader must be driven by internal cost, and every member of the team must be focused on cost. If the cost-driven leader and team were placed in a situation that was customer- and marketing-driven, they would have hard time adapting.

When the team, the organization, and the measurement and reward systems are not in sync, the strategy will either fail or be sub-optimized. Everything *must* fit together.

Step #4: Recognize that nothing lasts forever.

The old adage says, "If it ain't broke, don't fix it." Following that adage could be one of the fatal flaws for a successful company or business unit. If you have a winning strategy, leader, and team, there is a strong temptation to hold on, keep it in place, and assume it will continue to work. But following this path can lead to trouble, as shown in Exhibit 4.

Exhibit 4 – Nothing Lasts Forever

Waited Too Long To Change
- IBM stayed with caretaking/evolutionary management too long. It was slow to recognize the PC revolution, and then gave away the crown jewels and helped Microsoft and Intel become the leaders.
- GM stayed with caretaking, financially driven leaders. It invested in diversification instead of core businesses and refused to recognize importers and the importance of responding to customer needs.
- Kodak stayed with caretakers and product evolutionaries and missed the imaging revolution.

On The Job Too Long
- Peter Grace became a "legend in his own mind" while at the head of W. R. Grace.
- Ken Olsen stayed around too long at DEC and missed the micro market.
- An Wang made Wang a family business, but his son was not a leader.

Succession Planning Needed
- How long can Jack Welch continue to be successful at GE? Who will replace him?
- Are Microsoft, Intel, and other high fliers prepared for the next stage? It may come sooner than they think.

So when should you change leaders and teams? If a company has a strong handle on its markets and understands when a business or product line is moving from one stage of the life cycle to the next, it will be prepared to make the appropriate changes. Further, if it has a system of monitoring customer, technology, and competitive trends it will know the type of differentiator required to be the winner. The essence of strong strategic management is a combination of internal and external sensors that help to signal change and provide an early warning system to ensure that surprises are avoided and change is done systematically. This is what strategic leadership is designed to do.

The issue is whether the current management and team can be trained and prepared to change or whether a new leader and team are required. Some can make the transition, but they are rare. The preferable way is to bring in a new leader and team to make the necessary changes. It is like the platoon system in football – offensive and defensive teams. When the strategy changes, the team changes. The current team can then be moved to a new situation that can use its strengths.

Leaders and teams should be replaced in a systematic way. No leader should be in command more than eight to ten years. Leaders who remain in power too long begin to believe their own press releases and are often unwilling to make necessary changes or to turn over power to others.

Leaders must fit the strategic direction and life cycle of the business. They must have the ability and the commitment to implement the strategic differentiator, and they must have a time horizon that permits them to get the results, develop successors, and leave as winners.

3

Translating Strategic Thought into Action

Competing on Resources: Strategy in the 1990s

David J. Collis and Cynthia A. Montgomery

David J. Collis is an associate professor of business administration and Cynthia A. Montgomery is a professor of business administration at the Harvard Business School in Boston, Massachusetts. Their research focuses on corporate strategy and the competitiveness of diversified companies.

Source: *Harvard Business Review,* July-August 1995, pp. 118-128

A s recently as ten years ago, we thought we knew most of what we needed to know about strategy. Portfolio planning, the experience curve, PIMS, Porter's five forces – tools like these brought rigor and legitimacy to strategy at both the business-unit and the corporate level. Leading companies, such as General Electric, built large staffs that reflected growing confidence in the value of strategic planning. Strategy consulting boutiques expanded rapidly and achieved widespread recognition. How different the landscape looks today. The armies of planners have all but disappeared, swept away by the turbulence of the past decade. On multiple fronts, strategy has come under fire.

At the business-unit level, the pace of global competition and technological change has left managers struggling to keep up. As markets move faster and faster, managers complain that strategic planning is too static and too slow. Strategy has also become deeply problematic at the corporate level. In the 1980s, it turned out that corporations were often destroying value by owning the very divisions that had seemed to fit so nicely in their growth/share matrices. Threatened by smaller, less hierarchical competitors, many corporate stalwarts either suffered devastating setbacks (IBM, Digital, General Motors, and Westinghouse) or underwent dramatic transformation programs and internal reorganizations (GE and ABB). By the late 1980s, large multibusiness corporations were struggling to justify their existence.

Not surprisingly, waves of new approaches to strategy were proposed to address these multiple assaults on the premises of strategic planning. Many focused inward. The lessons from Tom Peters and Bob Waterman's "excellent" companies led the way, closely followed by total quality management strategy, reengineering, core competence, competing on capabilities, and the learning organization. Each approach made its contribution in turn, yet how any of them built on or refuted the previously accepted wisdom was unclear. The result: Each compounded the confusion about strategy that now besets managers.

A framework that has the potential to cut through much of this confusion is now emerging from the strategy field. The approach is grounded in economics, and it explains how a company's resources drive its performance in a dynamic competitive environment. Hence the umbrella term academics use to describe this work: the *resource-based view of the firm* (RBV).[1] The RBV combines the *internal* analysis of phenomena within companies (a preoccupation of many management gurus since the mid-1980s) with the *external* analysis of the industry and the competitive environment (the central focus of earlier strategy approaches). Thus the resource-based view builds on, but does not replace, the two previous broad approaches to strategy by *combining* internal and external perspectives.[2] It derives its strength from its ability to explain in clear managerial terms why some competitors are more profitable than others, how to put the idea of core competence into practice, and how to develop diversification strategies that make sense. The resource-based view, therefore, will be as powerful and as important to strategy in the 1990s as industry analysis was in the 1980s. (See the insert "A Brief History of Strategy.")

A Brief History of Strategy

The field of strategy has largely been shaped around a framework first conceived by Kenneth R. Andrews in his classic book *The Concept of Corporate Strategy* (Richard D. Irwin, 1971). Andrews defined strategy as the match between what a company *can* do (organizational strengths and weaknesses) within the universe of what it *might* do (environmental opportunities and threats).

Although the power of Andrews's framework was recognized from the start, managers were given few insights about how to assess either side of the equation systematically. The first important breakthrough came in Michael E. Porter's book *Competitive Strategy: Techniques for Analyzing Industries and Competitors* (Free Press, 1980). Porter's work built on the structure-conduct-performance paradigm of industrial-organization economics. The essence of the model is that the structure of an industry determines the state of competition within that industry and sets the context for companies' conduct – that is, their strategy. Most important, structural forces (which Porter called the five forces) determine the average profitability of the industry and have a correspondingly strong impact on the profitability of individual corporate strategies.

This analysis put the spotlight on choosing the "right industries" and, within them, the most attractive competitive positions. Although the model did not ignore the characteristics of individual companies, the emphasis was clearly on phenomena at the industry level.

With the appearance of the concepts of core competence and competing on capabilities, the pendulum swung dramatically in the other direction, moving from outside to inside the company. These approaches emphasized the importance both of the skills and collective learning embedded in an organization and of management's ability to marshal them. This view assumed that the roots of competitive advantage were inside the organization and that the adoption of new strategies was constrained by the current level of the company's resources. The external environment received little, if any, attention – and what

---

we had learned about industries and competitive analysis seemed to disappear from the collective psyche.

The emerging resource-based view of the firm helps to bridge these seemingly disparate approaches and to fulfill the promise of Andrews's framework. Like the capabilities approaches, the resource-based view shares another important characteristic with industry analysis. It, too, relies on economic reasoning. It sees capabilities and resources as the heart of a company's competitive position, subject to the interplay of three fundamental market forces: demand (does it meet customers' needs, and is it competitively superior?), scarcity (is it imitable or substitutable, and is it durable?), and appropriability (who owns the profits?). The five tests described in the article translate these general economic requirements into specific, actionable terms.

The RBV sees companies as very different collections of physical and intangible assets and capabilities. No two companies are alike because no two companies have had the same set of experiences, acquired the same assets and skills, or built the same organizational cultures. These assets and capabilities determine how efficiently and effectively a company performs its functional activities. Following this logic, a company will be positioned to succeed if it has the best and most appropriate stocks of resources for its business and strategy.

Valuable resources can take a variety of forms, including some overlooked by the narrower conceptions of core competence and capabilities. They can be *physical*, like the wire into your house. Potentially, both the telephone and cable companies are in a very strong position to succeed in the brave new world of interactive multimedia because they own the on-ramp to the information superhighway. Or valuable resources may be *intangible*, such as brand names or technological know-how. The Walt Disney Company, for example, holds a unique consumer franchise that makes Disney a success in a slew of businesses, from soft toys to theme parks to videos. Similarly, Sharp Corporation's knowledge of flat-panel display technology has enabled it to dominate the $7 billion worldwide liquid-crystal-display (LCD) business. Or the valuable resource may be an *organizational capability* embedded in a company's routines, processes, and culture. Take, for example, the skills of the Japanese automobile companies – first in low-cost, lean manufacturing; next in high-quality production; and then in fast product development. These capabilities, built up over time,

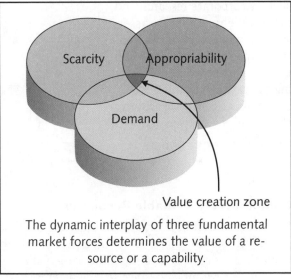

Value creation zone

The dynamic interplay of three fundamental market forces determines the value of a resource or a capability.

Figure 1. What Makes a Resource Valuable?

transform otherwise pedestrian or commodity inputs into superior products and make the companies that have developed them successful in the global market.

Competitive advantage, whatever its source, ultimately can be attributed to the ownership of a valuable resource that enables the company to perform activities better or more cheaply than competitors. Marks & Spencer, for example, possesses a range of resources that demonstrably yield it a competitive advantage in British retailing. (See the exhibit "How Marks & Spencer's Resources Give It Competitive Advantage.") This is true both at the single-business level and at the corporate level, where the valuable resources might reside in a particular function, such as corporate research and development, or in an asset, such as corporate brand identity. Superior performance will therefore be based on developing a competitively distinct set of resources and deploying them in a well-conceived strategy.

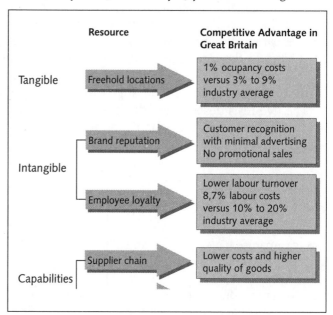

Figure 2. How Marks & Spencer's Resources
Give It Competitive Advantage

Competitively Valuable Resources

Resources cannot be evaluated in isolation, because their value is determined in the interplay with market forces. A resource that is valuable in a particular industry or at a particular time might fail to have the same value in a different industry or chronological context. For example, despite several attempts to brand lobsters, so far no one has been successful in doing so. A brand name was once very important in the personal computer industry, but it no longer is, as IBM has discovered at great cost. Thus the RBV inextricably links a company's internal capabilities (what it does well) and its external industry environment (what the market demands and what competitors offer). Described that way, competing on resources sounds simple. In practice, however, managers often have a hard time identifying and evaluating their companies' resources objectively. The RBV can help by bringing discipline to the often fuzzy and subjective process of assessing valuable resources.

For a resource to qualify as the basis for an effective strategy, it must pass a number of external market tests of its value. Some are so straightforward that most managers grasp them intuitively or even unconsciously. For instance, a valuable resource must contribute to the production of something customers want at a price they are willing to pay. Other tests are more subtle and, as a result, are commonly misunderstood or misapplied. These often turn out to cause strategies to misfire.

1. The test of inimitability: Is the resource hard to copy?

Inimitability is at the heart of value creation because it limits competition. If a resource is inimitable, then any profit stream it generates is more likely to be sustainable. Possessing a resource that competitors easily can copy generates only temporary value. But because managers fail to apply this test rigorously, they try to base long-term strategies on resources that are imitable. IBP, the first meat-packing company in the United States to modernize, built a set of assets (automated plants located in cattle-rearing states) and capabilities (low-cost "disassembly" of beef) that enabled it to earn returns of 1.3% in the 1970s. By the late 1980s, however, ConAgra and Cargill had replicated these resources, and IBP's returns fell to 0.4%.

Inimitability doesn't last forever. Competitors eventually will find ways to copy most valuable resources. But managers can forestall them – and sustain profits for a while – by building their strategies around resources that have at least one of the following four characteristics:

The first is *physical uniqueness,* which almost by definition cannot be copied. A wonderful real estate location, mineral rights, or Merck & Company's pharmaceutical patents simply cannot be imitated. Although managers may be tempted to think that many of their resources fall into this category, on close inspection, few do.

A greater number of resources cannot be imitated because of what economists call *path dependency.* Simply put, these resources are unique and, therefore, scarce because of all that has happened along the path taken in their accumulation. As a result, competitors cannot go out and buy these resources instantaneously. Instead, they must be built over time in ways that are difficult to accelerate.[3]

The Gerber Products Company brand name for baby food, for example, is potentially imitable. Recreating Gerber's brand loyalty, however, would take a very long time. Even if a competitor spent hundreds of millions of dollars promoting its baby food, it could not buy the trust that consumers associate with Gerber. That sort of brand connotation can be built only by marketing the product steadily for years, as Gerber has done. Similarly, crash R&D programs usually cannot replicate a successful technology when research findings cumulate. Having many researchers working in parallel cannot speed the process, because bottlenecks have to be solved sequentially. All this builds protection for the original resource.

The third source of inimitability is *causal ambiguity.* Would-be competitors are thwarted because it is impossible to disentangle either what the valuable resource is or how to re-create it. What *really* is the cause of Rubbermaid's continued success in plastic products? We can draw up lists of possible reasons. We can try, as any number of competitors have, to identify its recipe for innovation. But, in the final analysis, we cannot duplicate Rubbermaid's success.

Causally ambiguous resources are often organizational capabilities. These exist in a complex web of social interactions and may even depend critically on particular individuals. As Continental and United try to mimic Southwest's successful low-cost strategy, what will be most difficult for them to copy is not the planes, the routes, or the fast gate turnaround. All of those are readily observable and, in principle, easily duplicated. However, it will be difficult to reproduce Southwest's culture of fun, family, frugality, and focus because no one can quite specify exactly what it is or how it arose.

The final source of inimitability, *economic deterrence,* occurs when a company preempts a competitor by making a sizable investment in an asset. The competitor could replicate the resource but, because of limited market potential, chooses not to. This is most likely when strategies are built around large capital investments that are both scale sensitive and specific to a given market. For example, the minimum efficient scale for float-glass plants is so large that many markets can support only one such facility. Because such assets cannot be redeployed, they represent a credible commitment to stay and fight it out with competitors who try to replicate the investment. Faced with such a threat, potential imitators may choose not to duplicate the resource when the market is too small to support two players the size of the incumbent profitably. That is exactly what is now occurring in Eastern Europe. As companies rush to modernize, the first to build a float-glass facility in a country is likely to go unchallenged by competitors.

2. The test of durability: How quickly does this resource depreciate?

The longer lasting a resource is, the more valuable it will be. Like inimitability, this test asks whether the resource can sustain competitive advantage over time. While some industries are stable for years, managers today recognize that most are so dynamic that the value of resources depreciates quickly. Disney's brand name survived almost two decades of benign neglect between Walt Disney's death and the installation of Michael D. Eisner and his management team. In contrast, technological know-how in a fast-moving industry is a rapidly wasting asset, as the list of different companies that have dominated successive generations of semiconductor memories illustrates. Economist Joseph A. Schumpeter first recognized this phenomenon in the 1930s. He described waves of innovation that allow early movers to dominate the market and earn substantial profits. However, their valuable resources are soon imitated or surpassed by the next great innovation, and their superior profits turn out to be transitory. Schumpeter's description of major companies and whole industries blown away in a gale of "creative destruction" captures the pressure many managers feel today. Banking on the durability of most core competencies is risky. Most resources have a limited life and will earn only temporary profits.

3. The test of appropriability: Who captures the value that the resource creates?

Not all profits from a resource automatically flow to the company that "owns" the resource. In fact, the value is always subject to bargaining among a host of players, including customers, distributors, suppliers, and employees. What has happened to leveraged buyout firms is revealing. A critical resource of LBO firms was the network of contacts and relationships in the investment banking community. However, this resource often resided in the individuals doing the deals, not in the LBO firms as a whole. These individuals could – and often did – depart to set up their own LBO funds or move to another firm where they could reap a greater share of the profits that their resource generated. Basing a strategy on resources that are not inextricably bound to the company can make profits hard to capture.

4. The test of substitutability: Can a unique resource be trumped by a different resource?

Since Michael E. Porter's introduction of the five-forces framework, every strategist has been on the lookout for the potential impact of substitute products. The steel industry, for example, has lost a major market in beer cans to aluminum makers in the past 20 years. The resource-based view pushes this critical question down a level to the resources that underpin a company's ability to deliver a good or service. Consider the following example. In the early 1980s, People Express Airlines challenged the major airlines with a low-price strategy. Founder Donald C. Burr pursued this strategy by developing a unique no-frills approach and an infrastructure to deliver low-cost flights. Although the major airlines were unable to replicate this approach, they nevertheless were able to retaliate using a *different* resource to offer consumers equivalent low-cost fares – their computer reservation systems and yield-management skills. This substitution eventually drove People Express into bankruptcy and out of the industry.

5. The test of competitive superiority: Whose resource is really better?

Perhaps the greatest mistake managers make when evaluating their companies' resources is that they do not assess them relative to competitors'. Core competence has too often become a "feel good" exercise that no one fails. Every company can identify one activity that it does relatively better than other activities and claim that as its core competence. Unfortunately, core competence should not be an internal assessment of which activity, of all its activities, the company performs best. It should be a harsh external assessment of what it does better than competitors, for which the term *distinctive competence* is more appropriate. How many consumer packaged-goods companies assert that their core competence is consumer marketing skills? They may indeed all be good at that activity, but a corporate strategy built on such a core competence will rapidly run into trouble because other competitors with better skills will be pursuing the same strategy.

The way to avoid the vacuousness of generic statements of core competence is to disaggregate the corporation's resources. The category *consumer marketing skills,* for example, is too broad. But it can be divided into subcategories such as effective brand management, which in turn can be divided into skills such as product-line extensions, cost-effective couponing, and so on. Only by looking at this level of specificity can we understand the sources of a company's uniqueness and measure by analyzing the data whether it is competitively superior on those dimensions. Can anyone evaluate whether Kraft General Foods' or Unilever's consumer marketing skills are better? No. But we can demonstrate quantitatively which is more successful at launching product-line extensions.

Disaggregation is important not only for identifying truly distinctive resources but also for deriving actionable implications. How many companies have developed a statement of their core competencies and then have struggled to know what to do with it? One manufacturer of medical-diagnostics test equipment, for example, defined one of its core competencies as instrumentation. But this intuitively obvious definition was too broad to be actionable. By pushing to deeper levels of disaggregation, the company came to a powerful insight. In fact, its strength in instrumentation was mainly attributable to its competitive superiority in designing the interface between its machines and the people who use them. As a result, the company decided to reinforce its valuable capability by hiring ergonomists, and it expanded into doctors' offices, a fast-growing segment of its market. There, the company's resources created a real competitive advantage, in part because its equipment can be operated by office personnel rather than only by technicians.

Although disaggregation is the key to identifying competitively superior resources, sometimes the valuable resource is a combination of skills, none of which is superior by itself but which, when combined, make a better package. Honeywell's industrial automation systems are successful in the marketplace – a measure that the company is good at something. Yet each individual component and software program might not be the best available. Competitive superiority lies either in the weighted average (the company does not rank first in any resource, but it is still better on average than any competitor) or in its system-integration capability.

The lesson for managers is that conclusions about critical resources should be based on objective data from the market. In our experience, managers often treat core competence as an exercise in intuition and skip the thorough research and detailed analysis needed to get the right answer.

Strategic Implications

Managers should build their strategies on resources that meet the five tests outlined above. The best of these resources are often intangible, not physical, hence the emphasis in recent approaches on the softer aspects of corporate assets – the culture, the technology, and the transformational leader. The tests capture how market forces determine the value of resources. They force managers to look inward and outward at the same time.

However, most companies are not ideally positioned with competitively valuable resources. More likely, they have a mixed bag of resources – some good, some mediocre, and some outright liabilities, such as IBM's monolithic mainframe culture. The harsh truth is that most companies' resources do not pass the objective application of the market tests.

Even those companies that are fortunate enough to have unusual assets or capabilities are not home free. Valuable resources must still be joined with other resources and embedded in a set of functional policies and activities that distinguish the company's position in the market – after all, competitors can have core competencies, too.

Strategy requires managers to look forward as well. Companies fortunate enough to have a truly distinctive competence must also be wise enough to realize that its value is eroded by time and competition. Consider what happened to Xerox. During what has become known as its "lost decade," the 1970s, Xerox believed its reprographic capability to be inimitable. And while Xerox slept, Canon took over world leadership in photocopiers.

In a world of continuous change, companies need to maintain pressure constantly at the frontiers – building for the next round of competition. Managers must therefore continually invest in and upgrade their resources, however good those resources are today, and leverage them with effective strategies into attractive industries in which they can contribute to a competitive advantage.

What Ever Happened to the Dogs and Cash Cows?

In the late 1960s and early 1970s, the wisdom of the day was that companies could transfer the competitive advantage of professional management across a broad range of businesses. Many companies responded to the perceived opportunity. Armed with decentralized structures and limited, but tight, financial controls, they diversified into a number of related and unrelated businesses, mostly through acquisition. In time, such conglomerates came to resemble miniature economies in their own right. There appeared to be no compelling limits to the scope of corporations.

As the first oil crisis hit in 1973, corporate managers faced deteriorating performance and had little advice on how to act. Into this vacuum came the Boston
Consulting Group and portfolio management. In BCG's now famous growth/share
matrix, corporate management was finally given a tool with which to reassert
control over its many divisions.

The simple matrix allowed managers to classify each division, since renamed a
strategic business unit, into a quadrant based on the growth of its industry, and
the relative strength of the unit's competitive position. There was a prescribed
strategy for each position in the matrix: sustain the cash-generating cows, divest
or harvest the dogs, take cash from the cows and invest in question marks in order
to make them stars until their industry growth slowed and they became the next
generation of cash cows. Such simple prescriptions gave corporate management
both a sense of what their strategy should accomplish – a balanced portfolio of
business – and a way to control and allocate resources to their divisions.

The problem with the portfolio matrix was that it did not address how value
was being created across the divisions, which could be as diverse as semiconductors and hammers. The only relationship between them was cash. As we have
come to learn, the relatedness of businesses is at the heart of value creation in
diversified companies.

The portfolio matrix also suffered from its assumption that corporations had to
be self-sufficient in capital. That implied that they should find a use for all
internally generated cash and that they could not raise additional funds from the
capital market. The capital markets of the 1980s demonstrated the fallacy of such
assumptions.

In addition, the growth/share matrix failed to compare the competitive
advantage of business received from being owned by a particular company, with
the costs of owning it. In the 1980s many companies built enormous infrastruc-
tures that created only small gains at the business-unit level. During the same
period the market for corporate control heated up, focusing attention on value for
shareholders. Many companies with supposedly model portfolios were
accordingly dissolved.

Investing in Resources. Because all resources depreciate, an effective corporate strategy requires continual investment in order to maintain and build valuable resources. One of
Eisner's first actions as CEO at Disney was to revive the company's commitment to
animation. He invested $50 million in *Who Framed Roger Rabbit?* to create the company's
first animated feature-film hit in many years and quadrupled its output of animated
feature films – bringing out successive hits, such as *Beauty and the Beast, Aladdin,* and *The
Lion King.*

Similarly, Marks & Spencer has periodically re-examined its position in its only
business – retailing – and has made major investments to stay competitive. In the early
1980s, the British company spent billions on store renovation, opened new edge-of-town
locations, and updated its procurement and distribution systems. In contrast, the U.S.
retailer Sears, Roebuck and Company diversified into insurance, real estate, and stock

brokerages, while failing to keep up with the shift in retailing to new mall locations and specialty stores.

The mandate to reinvest in strategic resources may seem obvious. The great contribution of the core competence notion is its recognition that, in corporations with a traditional divisional structure, investment in the corporation's resources often takes a backseat to optimizing current divisional profitability. Core competence, therefore, identifies the critical role that the corporate office has to play as the guardian of what are, in essence, the crown jewels of the corporation. In some instances, such guardianship might even require explicitly establishing a corporate officer in charge of nurturing the critical resources. Cooper Industries, a diversified manufacturer, established a manufacturing services group to disseminate the best manufacturing practices throughout the company. The group helped "Cooperize" acquired companies, rationalizing and improving their production facilities. The head of the services group, Joseph R. Coppola, was of a caliber to be hired away as CEO of Giddings & Lewis, the largest U.S. machine tool manufacturer. Similarly, many professional service firms, such as Coopers & Lybrand, have a senior partner in charge of their critical capabilities – client-relationship management, staff training, and intellectual development. Valuable corporate resources are often supradivisional, and, unless someone is managing them on that basis, divisions will underinvest in them or free ride on them.

At the same time, investing in core competencies without examining the competitive dynamics that determine industry attractiveness is dangerous. By ignoring the marketplace, managers risk investing heavily in resources that will yield low returns. Masco Corporation did exactly that. It built a competence in metalworking and diversified into tightly related industries. Unfortunately, the returns from this strategy were lower than the company had expected. Why? A straightforward five-forces analysis would have revealed that the structure of the industries Masco entered was poor – buyers were price sensitive with limited switching costs, entry barriers were low, and suppliers were powerful. Despite Masco's metalworking expertise, its industry context prevented it from achieving exceptional returns until it developed the skills that enabled it to enter more attractive industries.

Similarly, if competitors are ignored, the profits that could result from a successful resource-based strategy will dissipate in the struggle to acquire those resources. Consider the value of the cable wire into your house as a source of competitive advantage in the multimedia industry. Companies such as Time Warner have been forced by competitors, who can also see the value of that wire, to bid billions of dollars to acquire control of even modest cable systems. As a result, they may never realize substantial returns on their investment. This is true not only for resources acquired on the market but also for those core competencies that many competitors are simultaneously trying to develop internally.

Upgrading Resources. What if a company has no unusually valuable resources? Unfortunately, that is a common experience when resources are evaluated against the standard of competitive superiority. Or what if a company's valuable resources have been imitated or substituted by competitors? Or perhaps its resources, like Masco's, are valuable only in industries so structurally unattractive that, regardless of how efficiently it operates, its financial returns will never be stellar. In these cases – indeed, in nearly all cases – companies must continually upgrade the number and quality of their resources and associated competitive positions in order to hold off the almost inevitable decay in their value.

Upgrading resources means moving beyond what the company is already good at, which can be accomplished in a number of ways. The first is by adding new resources, the way Intel Corporation added a brand name, Intel Inside, to its technological resource base. The second is by upgrading to alternative resources that are threatening the company's current capabilities. AT&T is trying to build capabilities in multimedia now that its physical infrastructure – the network – is no longer unique or as critical as it once was. Finally, a company can upgrade its resources in order to move into a structurally more attractive industry, the way Nucor Corporation, a U.S. steel company, has made the transition from competitive, low-margin, downstream businesses, such as steel joists, into more differentiated, upstream businesses, such as thin-slab cast-steel sheets.

Perhaps the most successful examples of upgrading resources are in companies that have added new competencies sequentially, often over extended periods of time. Sharp provides a wonderful illustration of how to exploit a virtuous circle of sequentially upgrading technologies and products, what the Japanese call "seeds and needs." In the late 1950s, Sharp was an assembler of televisions and radios, seemingly condemned to the second rank of Japanese consumer electronics companies. To break out of that position, founder Tokuji Hayakawa, who had always stressed the importance of innovation, created a corporate R&D facility. When the Japanese Ministry of International Trade and Industry blocked Sharp from designing computers, the company used its limited technology to produce the world's first digital calculator in 1964. To strengthen its position in this business, Sharp backward integrated into manufacturing its own specialized semiconductors and made a strong commitment to the new liquid-crystal-display technology. Sharp's bet on LCD technology paid off and enabled it to develop a number of new products, such as the Wizard electronic organizer. Over time, the superiority of its display technology gave Sharp a competitive advantage in businesses it had previously struggled in, such as camcorders. Its breakthrough product, Viewcam, captured 20% of the Japanese market within six months of release in 1992.

At each stage, Sharp took on a new challenge, whether to develop or improve a technology or to enter or attack a market. Success in each endeavor improved the company's resources in technology, distribution, and organizational capability. It also opened new avenues for expansion. Today, Sharp is the dominant player in the LCD market and a force in consumer electronics.

Cooper provides another example. Challenged to justify its plan to acquire Champion Spark Plug Company in 1989, when fuel injection was replacing spark plugs, Cooper reasoned that it had the resources to help Champion improve its position, as it had done many times before with products such as Crescent wrenches, Nicholson files, and Gardner-Denver mining equipment. But what really swung the decision, according to Cooper chairman and CEO Robert Cizik, was the recognition that Cooper lacked a critical skill it needed for the future – the ability to manage international manufacturing. With its numerous overseas plants, Champion offered Cooper the opportunity to acquire global management capabilities. The Champion acquisition, in Cizik's view, was a way to upgrade Cooper's resources. Indeed, a review of the company's history shows that Cooper has deliberately sought to improve its capabilities gradually by periodically taking on challenges it knows will have a high degree of difficulty for the organization.

Leveraging Resources. Corporate strategies must strive to leverage resources into all the markets in which those resources contribute to competitive advantage or to compete in new markets that improve the corporate resources. Or, preferably, both, as with Cooper's acquisition of Champion. Failure to do so, as occurred with Disney following the death of its founder, leads a company to be undervalued. Eisner's management team, which extended the scope of Disney's activities into hotels, retailing, and publishing, was installed in response to a hostile-takeover threat triggered by the under-utilization of the company's valuable resources.

Good corporate strategy, then, requires continual reassessment of the company's scope. The question strategists must ask is, How far can the company's valuable resource be extended across markets? The answer will vary widely because resources differ greatly in their specificity, from highly fungible resources (such as cash, many kinds of machinery, and general management skills) to much more specialized resources (such as expertise in narrow scientific disciplines and secret product formulas). Specialized resources often play a critical role in securing competitive advantage, but, because they are so specific, they lose value quickly when they are moved away from their original settings. Shell Oil Company's brand name, for example, will not transfer well outside autos and energy, however valuable it is within those fields. Highly fungible resources, on the other hand, transfer well across a wide range of markets but rarely constitute the key source of competitive advantage.

The RBV helps us understand why the track record of corporate diversification has been so poor and identifies three common and costly strategic errors companies make when they try to grow by leveraging resources. First, managers tend to overestimate the transferability of specific assets and capabilities. The irony is that because valuable resources are hard to imitate, the company itself may find it difficult to replicate them in new markets. Despite its great success in Great Britain, Marks & Spencer has failed repeatedly in attempts to leverage its resources in the North American market – a classic example of misjudging the important role that context plays in competitive advantage. In this case, the concepts of path dependency and causal ambiguity are both at work. Marks & Spencer's success is rooted in its 100-year reputation for excellence in Great Britain and in the skills and relationships that enable it to manage its domestic supply chain effectively. Just as British competitors have been unable to duplicate this set of advantages, Marks & Spencer itself struggles to do so when it tries to enter a new market against established competitors.

Second, managers overestimate their ability to compete in highly profitable industries. Such industries are often attractive precisely because entry barriers limit the number of competitors. Entry barriers are really resource barriers: The reason competitors find it so hard to enter the business is that accumulating the necessary resources is difficult. If it could be done easily, competitors would flock to the opportunity, driving down average returns. Many managers fail to see the connection between company-level resources and industry-level profits and convince themselves that they can vault the entry barrier, without considering which factors will ultimately determine success in the industry. Philip Morris Companies' entry into soft drinks, for example, foundered on the difficulties it faced managing the franchise distribution network. After years of poor performance in that business, it gave up and divested 7-Up.

The third common diversification mistake is to assume that leveraging generic resources, such as lean manufacturing, will be a major source of competitive advantage in a new market – regardless of the specific competitive dynamics of that market. Chrysler Corporation seems to have learned this lesson. Expecting that its skills in design and manufacturing would ensure success in the aerospace industry, Chrysler acquired Gulfstream Aerospace Corporation – only to divest it five years later in order to concentrate on its core businesses.

Despite the common pitfalls, the rewards for companies that leverage their resources appropriately, as Disney has, are high. Newell Company is another stunning example of a company that has built a set of capabilities and used them to secure commanding positions for products in a wide range of industries. Newell was a modest manufacturer of drapery hardware in 1967, when a new CEO, Daniel C. Ferguson, articulated its strategy: The company would specialize in high-volume production of a variety of household and office staple goods that would be sold through mass merchandisers. The company made a series of acquisitions, each of which benefited from Newell's capabilities – its focused control systems; its computer links with mass discounters, which facilitate paperless invoicing and automatic inventory restocking; and its expertise in the "good-better-best" merchandising of basic products, in which retailers typically choose to carry only one brand, with several quality and price levels. In turn, each acquisition gave Newell yet another opportunity to strengthen its capabilities. Today, Newell holds leading market positions in drapery hardware, cookware, glassware, paintbrushes, and office products and maintains an impressive 15% earnings growth annually. What differentiates this diversified company from a host of others is how it has been able to use its corporate resources to establish and maintain competitive advantage at the business-unit level.

However, even Newell benefits from the attractiveness of the markets in which it competes. All its products are infrequently purchased, low-cost items. Most consumers will not spend time comparison shopping for six glasses, nor do they have a sense of the market price. Do you know if $3.99 is too much to pay for a brass curtain rod? Thus Newell's resources are all the more valuable for being deployed in an attractive industry context.

Whether a company is building a strategy based on core competencies, is developing a learning organization, or is in the middle of a transformation process, those concepts can all be interpreted as a mandate to build a unique set of resources and capabilities. However, this must be done with a sharp eye on the dynamic industry context and competitive situation, rigorously applying market tests to those resources. Strategy that blends two powerful sets of insights about capabilities and competition represents an enduring logic that transcends management fads.

That this approach pays off is demonstrated by the impressive performance of companies such as Newell, Cooper, Disney, and Sharp. Although these companies may not have set out explicitly to craft resource-based strategies, they nonetheless capture the power of this logic and the returns that come to those who do.

Reference

1. A number of insightful articles have been written on the resource-based view, including: Birger Wernerfelt, "A Resource-Based View of the Firm," *Strategic Management Journal*, September-October 1984, p. 171; J.B. Barney, "Strategic Factor Markets: Expectations, Luck and Business Strategy," *Management Science*, October 1986, p. 1,231; Richard P. Rumelt, "Theory, Strategy, and Enterpreneurship," in *The Competivive Challenge: Strategies for Industrial Innovation and Renewal.* ed. David J. Teece (Cambridge, Mass.: Ballinger, 1987), p. 137; Ingemar Dierickx and Karel Cool, "Asset Stock Accumulation and Sustainability of Competitive Advantage," *Management Science*, December 1989, p. 1,504; Kathleen R. Conner, "A Historical Comparison of Resource-Based

Theory and Five Schools of Thought Within Industrial Organization Economics: Do We Have a New Theory of the Firm?" *Journal of Management*, March 1991, p. 121; Raphael Amit and Paul J.H. Schoemaker, "Strategic Assets and Organizational Rent," *Strategic Management Journal*, January 1993, p. 33; and Margaret A. Peteraf, "The Cornerstones of Competitive Advantage: A Resource-Based View," *Strategic Management Journal*, March 1993, p. 179.

2. To date, the most attention paid to the integration of the two perspectives has been by Michael E. Porter in *Competitive Advantage: Creating and Sustaining Superior Performance* (New York: Free Press, 1985) and, in the dynamic context, in his article "Towards a Dynamic Theory of Strategy," *Strategic Management Journal*, Winter 1991, p. 95.

3. These ideas were first discussed in two articles published in *Management Science*: Ingemar Dierickx and Karel Cool, "Asset Stock Accumulation and Sustainability of Competitive Advantage," December 1989, p. 1,504; and J.B. Barney, "Asset Stocks and Sustained Competitive Advantage," December 1989, p. 1,512.

Budgeting: From Pain to Power

Robert G. Finney

Robert G. Finney, a former president and CEO of Electronic Associates Inc., is author of "Powerful Budgeting for Better Planning & Management" (AMACOM, 1993).

Source: *Management Review,* September 1993, pp. 27-31.

At the sound of the word "budget," you can almost hear the silent groans. Across corporate America, few management words conjure up such negative emotions. Number crunching, belt tightening, slashing and burning. For these reasons, the much-maligned annual budget is frequently neglected when it should be a powerful management tool. In fact, it is one of a company's most useful planning documents. By not taking advantage of this potential force for better performance, companies create for themselves an unaffordable handicap in a competitive environment.

There are numerous inherent and manmade problems associated with budgeting that can make it a source of pain rather than satisfaction. In some companies, the budget is treated as a necessary evil. In others, it is approached with a curious mixture of disinterest and awe. "We only have a week to do this, so throw something together so we can get back to interesting work. By the way, you will not be allowed to exceed the costs in your budget next year, no matter what happens."

The inherent uncertainty of the future and the optimistic or pessimistic biases of different people make budgeting a multidimensional guessing game. Budgeting often consumes a number of months, both prolonging the pain and making the

---

Checklist for a Powerful Budgeting Process

- ✔ Is it realistic, accurate and internally consistent?
- ✔ Does it plan the best results achievable for the company that are consistent with acceptable risk and long-term health?
- ✔ Does it contain the information most useful to management?
- ✔ Is it consistent with a strategy that reassures employees that the company is moving in a good direction?
- ✔ Does it facilitate goal setting and measurement at all levels?
- ✔ Does it communicate operating plans, including support needs, across functions?
- ✔ Will it be beaten?
- ✔ Will it be approved?
- ✔ Does it give every organisation the resources it needs to meet its budgets?

predictions worse, because they are being made earlier. There is often such time pressure that managers cannot do sufficient research until some time during the next year when results are so far off budget that excruciating analysis begins.

Finally, budgets tend to be "cast in concrete." That semi-fictitious budget, conceived in haste, will haunt managers all year, and they probably will not be able to escape from the numbers on those pages.

So we have a process on which managers busily spend at least a quarter of the year, and whose results are often demonstrably wrong by the end of January. Is it not strange that businesses put up with this? Should stockholders have a warm feeling about such a budget, particularly when it is going to be the basis for management's decisions in the coming year?

Almost every manager in every business is involved in budgeting. That alone should make it an important management tool, but its value should be even greater. The budget expresses how available resources will be employed and deployed and what additional resources will be needed. It communicates where emphasis and priority will be placed and the performance sought. It should promulgate to all employees the all-important message that "management knows what it is doing." And it supplies all this information, not in the abstract, but in the specifics of people, dollars, equipment, orders, sales, profit and cash. In short, the budget is what gives a sense of reality to the company's objectives and strategies.

Accountants Need Not Apply

Budgeting is a management problem, not an accounting problem. The budget represents the plans for next year, revealing how management will seek its objectives and providing all the aspects of business mentioned above.

There are inherent problems, or obstacles, that make budgeting difficult even if the company is populated only with the best and brightest of people. The budget deals with the uncertain future, and many factors that dictate success or failure are outside factors beyond management's control. Because managers are measured on their performance against the budget, the managers directly on the firing line are not motivated to make their budget submissions challenging and realistic; they will strive for the most conservative budget that can get approved. All this makes budgeting essentially a psychological process, with "games" revolving around the inherent uncertainty and conflicts among participants.

The prerequisite for making the budget valuable, then, is to design a budgeting process that takes a behavioral approach to overcoming these obstacles while meeting budgeting objectives for all participants. The main objectives should be to plan the best performance realistically achievable, consistent with strategy, in the language most useful to management for operating, communicating and measuring performance. The budget must also give every organization within the company the resources it needs to accomplish what is expected. The obstacles cannot be avoided; the process must neutralize their effects.

Everything in the budgeting process must promote objectivity and concentration on the real opportunities and problems, rather than on "games." It must deal realistically with uncertainty and uncontrollability, removing these as a cause of confusion, and as an excuse for lower budgets or an excuse for later missing budgets. It must focus the entire organization on its most important parameters, rather than, for example, focusing on overhead rates when total costs are too high. And, since excellent performance never happens automatically, it should include a mechanism for promoting improvement and encouraging excellence throughout the company. The underlying principle must be "thinking it through" before "crunching the numbers."

Satisfaction of the following six requirements will allow budgeting to fulfill its potential:

- *Establish the context.* The budget must be prepared in the proper strategic context, within the framework of the company's objectives, strategies and plans. A planning continuum must be established leading from objectives and strategy to the finished budget. Content and timing must be integrated at every step.

  Four items must be incorporated in the budgeting process to establish the planning continuum: 1) the important outside environmental factors, those beyond the company's control that have a major bearing on its results; 2) the critical factors for success and related concerns; 3) a one-page summary strategy statement; and 4) preliminary budget numbers.

- *Deal with uncertainty and uncontrollability.* The process must deal realistically with factors that are uncertain and beyond management's control. Otherwise, it becomes impossible to tell whether management is doing a good job or is just lucky.

  No budget can be done without assumptions to handle the uncertain and uncontrollable, but they are often implicit, just carried along with the rest of the budget numbers. Making them explicit lets everyone understand what is controllable and subject to performance improvement, as well as the uncontrollable factors to which they may have to react. Explicit assumptions send a reassuring message to the organization that management understands the problems, and measurement and emphasis will be productive and fair.

BRIEFCASE

Budgeting does not have to be the onerous, unproductive task that it is in many companies. The annual budget is what gives a sense of reality to a company's objectives and strategies. It can and should be a powerful tool, leading to better management and better business performance. The guiding principle has to be "thinking it through" before "crunching the numbers."

The best way to make proper assumptions is an inside-out reasoning process. Start with the fundamental parameters of orders, sales, expense and cash flow, and decide what important factors in their determination are uncontrollable. Typical examples are customer financial problems that reduce orders and sales, material prices and interest rates. Then make numerical assumptions about those so identified. The important thing is not that the numerical assumptions turn out to be correct (If the experts cannot predict interest rates, how can we?), but the reasoning and the recognition that the factor is both uncontrollable and important.

PROBLEMS TO OVERCOME

1. Ensure that everything in the budgeting process promotes objectivity and concentration on the real strategy, opportunities and problems of the company.
2. Deal realistically with uncertainty and uncontrollability so that these are removed as a cause of confusion and as an excuse for lower budgets. They also need to be removed as a later excuse for missing the budget.
3. Focus the organization's attention on the parameters most important to performance and strategy and demand the best possible numerical predictions for all parameters.
4. Include a deliberate mechanism for promoting improvement and encouraging excellence throughout the company.

- *Select the format.* Management must select the format that provides the most useful information. The budget establishes the format for financial reviews throughout the year, and thus establishes the parameters on which the organization will focus.

  The most useful information for management is that which best portrays the benefits and consequences of its activities and actions. The budget format must 1) emphasize profit and cash flow directly; 2) focus on total costs, rather than on burdens and ratios; and 3) relate business outputs to activities.

  The budget format must not be driven by accounting's needs for financial reporting and auditing. In this computer age, it is easy to transform information, or to maintain it in two formats. For example, the outsourcing of paint shop activity always increases the labor overhead rate because it substitutes a purchase for direct labor. The overhead rate may be adequate for financial reporting purposes, but to make the right decision, management obviously needs to know the effects on total costs. A format emphasis on overhead rates, rather than total costs, can prevent the outsourcing question from ever getting on the table.

  The best format for a given business obviously depends on the specifics of that business. For many businesses, direct costing and activity-based costing are better than the traditionally popular gross margin/burden rate format.

- *Develop the content.* The content must provide the best possible numerical predictions of the next year's results. The budget deals with the unknown future, and the numbers that express expected performance are necessarily estimates. The task is to make sure these numerical entries are the most probable and meaningful that they can be.

  There are only three sources of budgeting estimates: direct data, trends and models. Good content requires good planning and understanding of the work to be done, plus proper use of these three sources.

  Direct data must not be stretched beyond the time it is valid. For example, a current order prospect is valid data for the short term, but 12 months hence probably will have either ordered or disappeared as a prospect. Trends must always be questioned before use; perhaps conditions that caused the trend have changed. Models are approximations but are a better source of predictions than invalid data or trends, particularly for types of businesses with large amounts of transactions, for which statistics and probabilities are useful.

- *Encourage excellence.* The process must encourage excellence and continuous performance improvement at all levels of the company. Management owes the stockholders the best performance possible. Because all the obstacles are arrayed against this objective, a deliberate technique is needed.

Gap analysis is an effective technique for this purpose. It begins with identification of a parameter of concern (from profit and cash flow for top management to skill levels or time to complete a repetitive task at lower levels) called the gap dimension. The desired goal level for this parameter is projected, as is the expected status quo result. The latter is the result of continuing to do things in the same way. The difference between these two projections defines a gap. The all-important final step is to develop action programs to fill the gap.

The beauty of gap analysis lies in the ways it can be applied, while giving participants a common language in which to deal objectively with goals, problems and actions. It is used in budgeting to decide and plan the most important actions throughout the company for the next year. These should be the essence of budgeting.

An organization should do only a small number of gap analyses; the purpose is to focus the organization's attention on important results. Too many gap analyses would defocus it.

- *Pay attention to process flow and details.* A coherent, efficient and timely process flow must tie everything together. A two-stage process is recommended. The first stage is "thinking it through." Strategies are communicated, planning done, and action programs developed. The second stage involves "crunching the numbers," generating all the details of the final budgets for all departments. The main output of the first stage is a preliminary budget, which 1) indicates whether chosen alternatives will yield a satisfactory budget, and 2) provides direction for the detailed work of the second stage. The preliminary budget is easier to change if budgeted results are inadequate. By contrast, if inadequate results are not evident until after number crunching, a huge amount of work has been wasted and will have to be re-done.

The details of the budgeting process must be carefully organized to ensure accuracy, consistency and communication throughout the company. The two main communication concerns are that every necessary interaction be covered consistently and that all elements of cost for a given activity be included. Clearly designating a capable budget analyst with coordinated responsibility and relying on the accounting department in general are good ways to promote the required communication.

Good budgeting leads to good management, which leads to good business performance. Good budgeting provides the information, focus and assured attitude required for good decisions, excellence and control in all activities, and intelligent and timely reaction to the problems and unpleasant surprises to which all businesses are subject. It can also directly aid downsizing, integration of a new acquisition, pricing, and "reengineering." The final benefit is the better results that follow the improved motivation and morale of the company.

WORKBOOK

If your company's budgeting is painful and you are in a position to change it, design a new budgeting process based on the six requirements in this article. It does not have to be done all at once – incremental benefits come from incremental effort.

If you are not in a position to change your company's process, here's how you can improve your own budgeting value and satisfaction:

1. Establish your own budgeting context from company and division strategies plans, and the desires of your boss.
2. Make your own explicit assumptions early in budgeting, carefully communicating them to your boss.
3. Develop and keep your own private budget format, if the company format does not give you the most useful information.
4. Properly use data, trends, models and input/output relationships to generate your numbers.
5. Establish your own private process to do the thinking early – the time pressure will probably be too great after company budgeting begins.

Strategy Implementation: the New Realities

Peter Lorange

Dr Peter Lorange is President and The Maucher Nestlé Professor, International Institute Management Development (IMD), Lausanne, Switzerland.

Source: *Long Range Planning,* Vol. 31, No. 1, 1998, pp. 18-29.

L atest trends indicate that human resources are becoming the key resource on which to focus the implementation of an organization's business strategy. More than ever before, new business growth is focused on the internal capabilities and resources of an organization rather than on a more traditional, acquisition-based drive. The driving forces for this internally-generated growth will include internal networking, project groups and *ad hoc* initiatives. As part of our discussion of new trends in strategy implementation, we will therefore propose a model for strategic planning that emphasizes team-based, internally-generated growth.

Whatever happened to those formal, long-range planning efforts that for so long constituted a major part of a firm's strategic implementation efforts? These formal, strategic plans, typical of the 60s, 70s and 80s, created clearly delineated, "divisionalized", hierarchical organizations with well-defined strategic business units. General Electric, for instance, was one of the most prominent examples of firms that followed this SBU-oriented approach.[1] Other well-documented examples are Beeton-Dickinson[2] and E.G.&G.[3] At that time, it was common to have a clear division of labor among executives at the various hierarchical levels in the organization. The Norton Corporation case[4] represents a clear example of this. Strategic planning within such a structure tended to be top-down *and* bottom-up. It was done on a regular, interactive – typically annual – basis. Needless to say, this kind of planning, and indeed this organizational form, assumed a certain stability in the business environment. It also assumed that there would be some degree of regularity in the way businesses were run as well as the reactions of competition, customers, etc. But, above all, the assumption was that capital was the critical, scarce strategic resource. So naturally, plans were heavily focused on free cash-flow, were made for steady expansion and were governed by the availability and flow of capital.

A New Reality for Strategic Planning

One reason why this traditional type of formal, strategic planning fell into disrepute was that it could easily "degenerate" into rather mechanical long-term extrapolation exercises.[5] The *people* in the organization were conspicuously absent from these types of plans!

Today, the reality of strategic planning and strategy implementation has changed and so has the job of the strategic planner, but for *different* reasons than those traditionally put forward. Nowadays, the strategic planner, as *chief implementation officer*, needs a different focus and so do the management processes he must work with, for the following reasons:

- *The knowledge-based organization.* People, not financial resources, are becoming the key strategic resource. The focus of effective strategy implementation today should above all be on how to utilize the relevant know-how of key people in the organization in the best possible way – i.e. how to "allocate" them to the most useful tasks in order to achieve effective implementation – the so-called resource-based view.[6] Management processes should also reflect this reality.

- In today's knowledge-based organizations the *interplay* between the strategic planner and the human resource manager is vital. In fact, in many organizations, it may be difficult to distinguish between the functions of strategic planning and human resource management because, in a knowledge-based organization, they should work as a team.

- Today's relatively "flat", re-engineered, typically heavily-networked organizations require a new kind of strategy implementation. Contrary to the traditional approach, now there is less strategic planning and implementation through the formal operating organization. Increasingly, strategic initiatives are referred to task forces on a project-by-project basis. Fewer strategic plans are being articulated, at least in a formal way, by operating entities. Instead, operating line members are *also* being included in *ad hoc,* strategic initiative implementation teams.

- Planning staffs, at least as defined in the classical sense as "the coordinators of formal strategic plans", are getting smaller and smaller and in some cases, disappearing altogether. Taking their place is a new breed of planning staff that can be found at the interface of the project management support and human resource management functions. The job of this new planning cadre is to help staff-critical, strategic projects by providing the most appropriate human resources at each stage.

- The nature of strategic planning, if we accept a definition of it as a "continuously changing portfolio of projects evolving towards completion", *implies that the strategies themselves are becoming increasingly incremental,* based on the learning that is taking place around each strategic project. As the knowledge base in the organization improves, strategies are thus being continuously redefined. Consequently, as formal plans cannot be long-lived, it is perhaps no longer useful to articulate a full-bodied strategic plan as it, too, will continuously change as the content of the strategic programs are revised.

Focus on Internally-Generated Growth

In the recent past, the major strategic focus has emphasized restructuring and re-engineering.[7] Norsk Hydro, for instance, embarked upon its "Hydro Plus" in 1994. Initially, it was aimed at reducing costs, adding organizational focus and stimulating new business growth. While the program succeeded in bringing down costs, reducing head count and simplifying the organization, it proved difficult simultaneously to enhance internally-generated growth. Rockwool International represents one of many similar cases.[8]

The aim was to achieve leaner, more efficient value creation in the various parts of an organization. But an unintended side-effect has been a restriction of the organization's abilities to pursue internally-generated growth. Relatively speaking, too much emphasis was put on cutting costs, rather than using the organization's key resources to experiment with or pursue new business opportunities, to build a business for the future. Today, the pendulum seems to have swung the other way. Managers recognize that the maximum utilization of a firm's resources *does* call for the use of the key strategic resource, the key people/talents, in a way that allows them to create new business through internally-generated growth. Over the last decade, Nestlé, for example, achieved 70% of its growth from acquisitions. Now it aims at achieving 70% of its growth during the next ten years via internally-generated business, with particular emphasis on four knowledge-based dimensions:[9]

- Rapid dissemination of new ideas within Nestlé's global network of key executives – trying to circumvent the frequent "not-invented-here" syndrome.

- Including a much higher proportion of proprietary know-how in new products – thus also creating a basis for setting the company apart from competition.

- Focusing on applying pertinent cutting-edge know-how as it applies to new channels of distribution.

- Shifting the cost focus from achieving lowest cost products to lowest cost provider to the customer, i.e. applying a broader value-chain know-how, inspired by open systems thinking.

Thus, at Nestlé for instance, *specific* knowledge-based organizational initiatives have been set in motion to make this strategic shift happen.

This drive toward internally-generated growth has been further accentuated by the fact that opportunities for acquisitions have become less obvious. The price for good acquisition candidates has risen steadily and the number of remaining qualified ones has become increasingly limited. Take, for example, the recent acquisitions and mergers that are taking place in the chemicals industry, with ICI purchasing Unilever's specialty chemicals for a record price of £4.9 billion, while simultaneously selling its basic chemicals business to DuPont for another record sum of £2 billion. Look also at Shell's purchase of Montedison's stake in Montell, as well as Borealis's takeover of PCD petrochemicals as part of an equity swap, all transactions reflecting very high valuations. Similarly Hoffmann-La Roche rushed to take over Boehringer/Ingelheim and Tastemakers, both at high price/earnings multiples. These and many other recent examples of transactions seem to lead to industry consolidation, with fewer and fewer remaining target entities available for purchase.

In large, diversified companies, the chief executive officer and his chief financial staff typically play a major role in acquisition-based growth, and strategic planning is part of this process. With a shift toward internally-generated growth, the CEO will need a broader set of staff support. Today's strategic planners therefore have more of a coaching role, motivating the organization to pursue new business opportunities for growth. In fact, they have taken on the increasingly important role of catalysts for internal growth and increasingly the custodians of the firm's entrepreneurial drive. So, their first priority must be effectively to fulfil this vital function of building on the initiatives and talents of key people in the organization. On the assumption that "strategy means choice", the specific challenge for strategic planners is how to give the people in the organization a chance to contribute where the payoff is the highest, not to be sidelined by less essential activities.

What Can Inhibit Growth?

Today's strategic planners thus have to take another look at "growth". It has shifted from being typically supply-driven to being much more demand-driven. What matters now is having a better feel for what major customer segments might want – almost guiding them towards new needs that they might not yet even be aware of! The company that can meet such an emergent customer need will often ride on strong waves of demands, experiencing that "the winner takes all"! In this context, the understanding of emerging customer needs and where these are coupled with purchasing power, are becoming critical. The growth of the cellular telephone business is a case in point. One of the most critical skills in the future will be understanding demographics and economic growth, in particular as it applies to emerging markets.[10] Future growth implies looking outside the classical European-North American-Japanese trio. L. M. Ericsson's fastest growing market recently has been mainland China, which now ranks as its 4th largest. Japanese auto makers, for example, were fast to tap the huge emerging growth potential in the Southeast Asian market. Nestlé's strongest growth in Europe is in Russia, as well as stronger-than-average growth in most of the former Eastern Bloc countries. Fiat's early move into Poland has led it to enjoy exceptional growth. All these examples – and many others – are fundamentally demand-driven, tapping potentially large unsaturated customer needs.

To understand these changes toward demand-driven growth, it is essential to comprehend the effects of the entire population mix – the young and the aging – particularly the concomitant purchasing and task shifts. Some segments are ready to be served on a large scale already – those where needs and purchasing power coincide. Others can be addressed in an economically realistic way, so that they can provide the basis for strong growth when they achieve more purchasing power in the future. It is necessary to have an intimate understanding of these shifts on a global basis. Moreover, as the radically changing nature of communications turns the world into a "global village", there are further startling changes ahead in the challenges of growth. New consumer trends now spread much faster, calling for corporations to manage global brands and images much more carefully as diffusion time for new product introductions to all parts of the world becomes shorter and shorter.

Despite the potential of internal, growth-driven strategy, the strategic planner will, nevertheless, have to face a number of possibly serious obstacles to implementation:

- *Lack of a true growth culture in the organization, from top to bottom.* The chief executive officer himself must be out front promoting internally-generated growth. This may mean, in particular, that the CEO and his close executives will have to *listen* much more carefully to key customers as well as to members of his organization who are able to spot new opportunities. But this will have to be skillful, insightful listening, to avoid the pitfall pointed out by Akin Morita, founder and former CEO of Sony: "If you survey the public for what they think they need, you'll always be behind in this world. You'll never catch up unless you think one to ten years in advance and create a market for the items you think the public will accept at that time".[11]

- *Too much organizational complexity.* In many established businesses, this can result in a gradual build-up of overly-complicated product ranges and distribution systems, which can provide too much negative ballast for the organization. If too much energy is spent on extending the life of mature products, as well as on *ad hoc* mini-crises and fire-fighting, there will be too few possibilities to focus on simple, new ideas for growth.

Here, it is interesting to see how leading companies almost "intentionally" accelerate the obsolescence of old products, to create space for new ones. For instance, at Matsushita, the consumer electronics giant, 50% of its product range is three years old or less!

- *Strong organizational kingdoms.* Even though we are living in an age of flat, project-based organizations, strong remnants of the traditional "kingdom creating" still abound. Such kingdoms can limit the full utilization of an organization's potential. The inability or unwillingness of company executives to break out of their parochial ways can be a critical impediment against growth. There are numerous examples of this, perhaps most typically revealed when companies have been through a recent merger and are faced with achieving post-merger integration for growth.

- *Lack of speed and urgency.* In today's markets, where the winner seems to take all, it is insufficient to be market-driven – the winners are the market-drivers. Take, for instance, the race within the automotive industry to bring out new models faster and on a global scale. Five years ago, it took, on average, 48 months to develop a new so-called car platform; today, it takes only 32 to 36 months.

- *Lack of tradition-breaking.* The key is to be innovative, to break out of the old, conventional modes of doing things. Unfortunately, many organizations do not allow themselves to do this. Experimentation, risk-taking – even in the smallest form – is not permissible. A rather dramatic example of tradition-breaking is General Motors International's development of its standardized global plant, radically different from anything seen before, incorporating strong sub-supplier networking. Four such plants are being built – in record time – in such diverse places as Argentina, Poland, Thailand and China.[12] To ensure maximum leverage from its enzyme technology and other cutting-edge nutritional know-how, Nestlé has established a new division, reporting directly to its President/CEO, not in the least to ensure that the new technology leads to maximum leverage – again, tradition-breaking!

- *Lack of cost competitiveness.* Needless to say, cost competitiveness, based on a constant "good can always be done even better" effort, *must* be an essential condition for growth. In a properly re-engineered world, growth becomes a *complement* to cost competitiveness, not an alternative. The General Motors example cited above is a case in point.

A Model for Thinking About Growth

Let us now discuss a model for strategic business development originally developed by Chakravarthy and Lorange.[13] The strategic planner, in his role as a catalyst for growth, may now want to reflect on two critical issues:

- First, how to sharpen the focus on finding business opportunities that are not obvious to everybody else. How to encourage curiosity, experimenting, prudent risk-taking, i.e. the joy and excitement of taking on new challenges when it comes to serving the customer in new ways – perhaps even by focusing on new needs that the customer himself does not yet see!

- Second, how to sharpen effective implementation, focusing on delineating and mobilizing task forces for pursuing such opportunities? This will mean encouraging flexibility, comfort in working in "flat" organizations, thriving on constant change, being comfortable with a certain degree of ambiguity and a multiplicity of roles, i.e., wearing several hats. For the strategic planner, an intimate understanding of *who* is capable of doing *what* among the people in his company will thus be essential and therefore close co-operation with the human resource function will be necessary.

For the planner, addressing these two issues amounts to playing a dual role, that of the *entrepreneur* and that of the *organizational developer.* These two roles, or central concerns, are illustrated in the model in Fig. 1. The model has an entrepreneurial dimension (see the vertical axis), focusing on questions the planner should ask to determine where the firm is and where it needs to go:

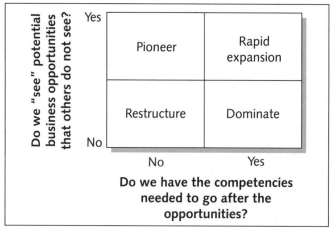

Source: Dr. Balaji Chakravarthy and Dr. Peter Lorange, *Managing the Strategic Process: A Framework for a Multibusiness Firm*, Prentice Hall, Englewood Cliffs, N.J., 1991

Figure 1. A strategic approach for internally generated growth

- Do we see potential business opportunities that others do not yet see? The answer to this can be yes or no, or usually somewhere in between. Needless to say, many of the business activities a firm pursues are also seen by other companies, typically major competitors. Still, it is worthwhile to single out the newer opportunities that are not yet part of the main stream of the business sector. The reason is that it is exactly here that entrepreneurial growth opportunities can most likely be found.

The model also has a second dimension, organizational development/human resource (see the horizontal axis). This can be delineated by means of the following question:

- Do we have the organizational competencies needed to go after each identified opportunity? Again, the answer can be affirmative when we have the appropriate team and mobilized the adequate human resources. The answer can also be, no; we do not yet have the resources at hand – they need to be assembled by searching for them in various parts of the organization, "discovering our own talents" and searching for them outside to build the required team.

From Fig. 1, we can see that, depending on the answers to the two above questions, it may be useful to think about four kinds of strategic challenges, i.e. four strategic contexts. How the strategic challenges for a company – and its strategic planners – will be articulated in terms of the focus for each strategic archetype mentioned in Fig. 1 will thus depend on how it answers the two questions.

- *Pioneer.* Here we may see a potential business opportunity, but we need to test it further and we do not yet have the organizational capabilities to exploit it. In this case, the challenge is experimentation, a willingness to try to define a new business in a new holistic sense, with an aim to come up with a viable way to serve the customer in new ways, perhaps not yet recognized by the customer himself!

- *Rapid Expansion.* In this quadrant, management and planners feel that a unique opportunity does indeed seem to exist and they are also in the envious position of having the people and talents ready to go after the opportunity. In this case, rapid expansion should be the aim, doing everything possible to take advantage of the situation and focusing on finding the *right path* to pursue such rapid business progress.

- *Dominate.* This is the most common strategic situation. Here, the challenge is to come up with a competitive strategy, based on differentiation and/or cost advantages relative to competitors, in order to dominate a certain business area. Building/defending market shares is vital. Continuous focus on incremental improvements to "make good even better" will be critical here – all the time willing to re-engineer one's value-creating activities. A question to be kept in mind, however, is: Where did the business initially come from? How did this business position initially get established? Perhaps the answer can be found in earlier Pioneer and Rapid Expansion modes – the construction of business positions that can later be the basis for domination and defending one's positions. Competition-dominating strategies can thus often be best defended by developing new related Pioneer/Rapid Expansion initiatives – i.e. a vibrant front-end strategic pipeline! Cost-cutting and re-engineering of dominant business positions alone are not likely to be enough successfully to defend most businesses in today's world of rapid change.

- *Restructure.* Here, the business typically is in a degree of trouble, with a call for both redefining what the organization should be doing and realigning to do it. Above all, the challenge here is not to throw away useful knowledge that can be a basis for future growth when realigned. Too often, the restructuring/right-sizing efforts lead to the perhaps unintentional discarding of know-how that could have been used for future growth in another context. While the focus on restructuring is important, we shall not discuss it further in this article, but rather concentrate our arguments on the "front end" of new business development – Pioneering, which, with some degree of likelihood, might lead to Rapid [business] Expansion – and how this might link into a subsequent "Dominate" position for the business.

A Tailored Approach to Growth

While we believe that the formal planning systems of the past are no longer as applicable, it is still useful and necessary to provide some sort of strategic process support for internally-generated, growth-driven, strategy implementation. We recommend five areas where a tailored set of guidelines can be useful.

These guidelines should therefore be considered as propositions for strengthening the present planning and control systems. Above all, it will be seen that behavioral issues, as well as adding more focus on organizational capabilities and competencies, are called for.

Guideline 1: *How to identify and articulate the main strategic tasks.* For each of the three strategic dimensions (Pioneer, Rapid Expansion and Dominate), Fig. 2 lists key questions that the strategic teams, who will develop and implement these strategies, will have to address. The planning process should thus be modified so that these types of questions are added to the protocol/formats for articulating business plans. Often this is not the case, however, with issues relating solely to dominate-type competitive strategies being included.

	Pioneer	Rapid Expansion	Dominate
Team Task Focus	• Identify opportunities • Create new business concepts with visionary customer • Value-driven R in R&D	• Mobilize for expansion to preempt competitors • Make iterative changes to find right strategic path • More D than R in R&D! – incremental relaunches	• Make good even better • Fulfill needs through process innovation • Value to customer • Price aggressively

Figure 2. How to identify and anticipate strategic tasks

Guideline 2: *The composition of the management team.* Figure 3 lists the most appropriate people, constellations, focuses and assignments for each of the implementation task forces (Pioneer, Rapid Expansion and Dominate). The key is thus to recognize that it is *people* – typically working in teams – that make strategies become realities. To identify who is involved in what and when, should therefore be an integral step in the strategic planning process. Furthermore, a special tailoring emphasis should be pursued, to get the most appropriate team chemistry for each strategic task. As noted earlier, close co-operation with the human resources function will thus be called for, even to the extent of integrating the strategic planning and the human resource management systems.

	Pioneer	Rapid Expansion	Dominate
Team Composition and Focus	• Creative • Diverse representation, complementary strengths and skills • Brainstormers • Entrepreneurial mind	• Doers – finding workable path • "Experimenters" • One team, with specialists • Temporary assignments – modified as necessary	• Classical, discipline-based teams • Cost and quality focus • Deliver bottom-line results aggressively

Figure 3. Composition of the management team

Guideline 3: *The team's dominant learning mode.* It should be pointed out here that learning, in order to accumulate more relevant strategic knowledge, should be at the center of a firm's strategic implementation efforts. Hence, a formalized approach to learning for executives may be called for. Typically, progress is primarily assessed through budget-based control. It is doubtful, however, whether budget deviation actually can shed a deeper insight into why the strategic progress took a certain path or another, particularly when it comes to the Pioneer and Rapid Expansion contexts. Figure 4 suggests several organizational learning modes that we recommend be integrated into control process.

	Pioneer	Rapid Expansion	Dominate
Team Dominant Learning Mode	● Holistic – "child-like" approach to conceptualizing a business – **Piaget**	● Path-finder – how to realistically scale up the business – **Leavitt**	● Incremental – provide ongoing improvements and more value to customer – **Descartes**

Figure 4. Dominant learning modes

Several of the pioneers of learning in social science can provide useful lenses through which to consider how learning in each of the three strategic archetype stages needs to operate. The essence of organizational learning in the Pioneer context may be quite similar to the learning processes in children, when they gradually develop a certain understanding. Piaget theorized that children adapt their experiences with objects into increasingly sophisticated cognitive models that enable them to deal with future situations in more effective ways.[14] Similarly, the organization may develop an increasingly sophisticated view of the pioneer business strategy as it abandons more primitive, premature views. Likewise, the "Rapid Expansion" mode could be likened to a pathfinder type of learning, as discussed by Harold Leavitt, the Stanford-based psychologist.[15] The key is to abandon blind paths in the search for the most easily travelled path for Rapid Expansion – a tried and tested approach! Finally, learning in the Dominate mode can perhaps be compared with the type of learning, analyzing and understanding what Descartes proposed: splitting a phenomenon apart into separate pieces, then putting it together again in a holistic sense. [16] Deviations relative to the partial understanding of the pieces might then create learning.

Guideline 4: *Top management's mode for reviewing strategic plans.* Realistic planning processes must allow for inputs from and participation of many executives. This is essential to create realistic plans that the organization will be committed to. Thus, developing a cohesive corporate-wide plan requires top-down/bottom-up interaction across several organizational levels and also typically several iterations. Figure 5 provides an overview of how top management might interact with the various strategy implementation teams in planning these interfaces.

	Pioneer	Rapid Expansion	Dominate
Top Management's Strategy Review Focus	Allow for *experimentation* • "sit down and think together" • Stimulate curiosity • Longer term focus • Risk-taking	Multiple-expansion *scenarios* • which path is best? • Modify until the best team is in place	Clear *competitive* focus • "Bottom line to be defended" • "Good can be done better" • Shorter term focus

Figure 5. Top management's mode of interaction with strategy implementation team

We are suggesting that top management needs to *tailor* its approach. Why? Because the rest of the organization often perceives the chief executive officer and his closest team with a sense of "power distance". Also, with typically impressive trade records behind them many of them may become rather self-confident about their own capabilities and may not actually see the need for a more flexible approach. In such cases, we recommend that: with pioneering activities, the CEO and the top management team should be near the rest of the organization, almost part of the pioneering teams themselves. They should act as a resource to these teams, allow access to their usually considerable network of outside contacts, encourage and instill fighting spirit when things are not going as smoothly as desired – in other words, a catalyst role. When interacting with rapid expansion activities, the distance should be greater. Here, the CEO and top management should attempt to stimulate analysis of whether the particular team behind this strategic initiative is on the best-possible path to realistic, fast business scale-up. Strong analytical support to the rapid expansion team can be an important contribution to success. When it comes to interacting with dominate activities, the distance is typically the farthest away. Here, the CEO's top-down strategic vision to demonstrate commitment to shorter-term performance is likely to be strong. To summarize the role of top management in the strategy implementation process, we can see the need for top-level tailor-making, interacting and iterating rather as a *catalyst* in the pioneer strategy, *analyst* vis-à-vis the rapid expansion and *strategist* vis-à-vis the dominate strategy.

Guideline 5: *Strategic control modes*. Finally, Fig. 6 indicates a range of possible strategic control modes to add flexibility and tailored strategic focus to the management control process.[17] Here, a "go/no go" control approach may be called for vis-à-vis the Pioneer mode. The challenge here is to control the pioneer activity in an analogous way to an experiment. After a finite amount of time has gone by and the pioneer "experiment" has been operating within pre-specified resource limits for people and funds, it will be the time to assess whether one has a new business concept or not. Typically, an unfortunate lack of "go-no go" focus can lead the pioneering projects to drift.

	Pioneer	Rapid Expansion	Dominate
Management Control Mode	*Go / no go* • "either we take the business or not"	*Contingent control* • "either we stick to the projected scenario or we change path"	*Steering control* • "budget deviations must lead to incremental corrective actions"

Figure 6. Different strategic control modes

Similarly, some sort of contingent control (or scenario control) may be necessary when dealing with the Rapid Expansion mode to check whether or the directional development of the business is on the right track. If it is not on a workable path, the scenario may have to be changed. When it comes to the Dominate stage, where business direction has been well-established, then conventional budget-based deviation control techniques may be very effective. A strong classical control approach is indeed essential here. However, during the development of new business activities, the application of uniform strategic controls based on classical budgetary methods, will probably be ineffective. In fact, unilaterally applied, well-intentioned, but misguided, budgetary control activities can represent a major impediment to successful Pioneer and/or Rapid Expansion strategic developments for rapid growth.

We see from all the above examples that the key challenges for making the strategy process work in this new context – and hence the five areas of process modifications which we suggested – have mostly to do with the added striving for internal growth. This motivation can in all likelihood only be achieved by instilling an added human resource emphasis, i.e. an ability to mobilize relevant teams, behind *ad hoc* project plans, depending on the strategic mode and an ability to tailor formal planning, control and human resource efforts according to the strategic context.

What is the Overall Strategic Portfolio?

In the past, there has been a strong tradition within strategy practice to place considerable emphasis on the overall strategic portfolio. Planning would thus emphasize mature vs. growth divisions, cash flow generation vs. usage considerations cyclical/counter cyclical patterns, geographical spread of the portfolio, etc. In the present competence-based approach, the focus is much more on having an overall strategic portfolio of activities that represents a blend, a balance of human resources and human capabilities. Thus the portfolio would need to be based on:

• An ample set of capabilities related to being able to deliver on entrepreneurial pioneering,

• Another set of capabilities linked to the ability to execute on scaling-up in order to aggressively grow the new business,

• And finally another set of capabilities in order to perform well within the more classical competitive situations where one reaps benefits from domination and defense of one's business positions.

With this added way of establishing a portfolio focus, top management might have to reassess the overall portfolio picture based on the strategic initiatives of the firm. A first step might be to plot the various strategic projects onto a chart such as Fig. 1. Management then should ask the question: Do we seem to have an appropriate balance between the activities going on within Pioneer, Rapid Expansion and Dominate modes? Typically, such a portfolio assessment will reveal whether there are enough "front-end" activities in the business pipeline of the organization or not. Often, this type of portfolio assessment reveals a relatively weak Pioneer/Rapid Expansion side in the portfolio, suggesting that relatively more resources should be used today for the future, both in the form of Pioneering activities and Rapid Expansion activities.

Since many Pioneer activities will, in fact, not materialize, it is important to realize that a relatively large number of such strategic initiatives are desirable for getting the desired payoffs from the Pioneer mode. The Rapid Expansion mode would fall in between simply because one cannot generally afford to expand every possible pioneer activity. Some pioneer activities deserve to be abandoned, so that the bulk of the resources can be put into action where they really have major, potential payoffs. Strategy means *choice* and the key choices focus on how to deploy human resources to achieve a strong overall strategic portfolio.

Dynamic Change in Positioning Among the Strategic Modes

A key task for top management and strategic planners will be to assess *when* a strategic initiative should be "reclassified" from one mode to another. For such an assessment, several questions need to be asked:

- *When do we formally establish a pioneer activity?* Clearly, "pre-pioneer" initiatives will abound. So, a major question is: When do we formalize a pioneer activity by allocating organizational resources to it? Senior management must play a central role here. The key issues to be addressed are: Does the basic proposition reveal a sensible new business idea? How is the customer to be served differently? What might be the new value/attraction for the customer? It is also incumbent upon top management to assess the personal capabilities, strengths and track records of those who propose pioneering activities. In addition, management may also want to seek a broader set of opinions from various sources that might have insights on the customers to be served, basic technological questions, etc. As we said earlier, it is important to allow pioneering to take place; it would thus be undesirable to let excessive analysis lead to the termination of possibly fertile projects before they can get a chance to prove that they might bear fruit. The key is to allow for risk-taking and unorthodox initiatives; to let people be creative by sticking their necks out. It is unfortunately all too easy to shoot any such project down; top management must guard against this.

- *Moving from pioneer to rapid expansion.* Here again, top management needs to be involved. The questions they should be asking are: When do we have a reasonable confirmation that we have a viable new business proposition? When do we need to stop further experimentation or to pursue the idea to its fullest extent? Can we now more clearly see a market and potential revenue stream? Above all, do we now seem to have sufficient organizational capabilities and competencies in place to be realistically able to scale up? Do we feel confident about *who* will do *what?* Projects that create a lot of doubt, procrastination and second-guessing as to whether they rest on a solid business concept or not, should probably be set aside. Top management needs to be able to drop projects that do not seem to have plausible potential, as too many sub-standard, Pioneer activities can divert key human resources from other, high priority activities. Again, safeguarding the use of core organizational resources will be essential – *strategy means choice!*

- *When is a rapid expansion project no longer viable and should be redefined or closed down?* The key to this depends on whether a workable way of scaling up the business is found or not. To switch from one alternative scenario for scaling up to another can indeed become quite expensive. One should think about this as similar to the exponential increase in costs when going from pre-clinical trial to clinical testing of drugs. When clinical testing does not work out, the drug being tested is normally abandoned. Only in some cases does this lead to a reformulation of the drug and renewed clinical testing. Usually, the drug is dropped. Similarly, when Rapid Expansion efforts run into major problems, management needs to decide if it is time to abort, rather than put more organizational resources into a major refocusing of the effort.

- *When does a rapid expansion situation mature into a dominate/defend position?* The answer largely depends on how fast major competitors are coming in with copy strategies or with new generations of the same type of product or service. Management then needs to modify the strategy into one with more focus on intruding competitors. One is no longer alone. Attention to competitive pricing will be vital – and so will availability and service to the trade. In short, this is the time to redefine the rapid expansion strategy into a more conventional one, following classical competitive strategy approaches.

What are the New Roles for the Key Actors in Strategy Implementation?

Top Management

We have seen that top management will typically have to play a very important role in various strategic project initiatives when following this human competence-based approach. After all, we are dealing with the firm's most talented pool of people and thus with potential interpersonal conflicts between strong egos, stemming from strategic assignment choices. This requires resolution at the top! Indeed, management efforts have to be tailor-made according to what is needed to succeed in a Pioneer vs. a Rapid Expansion or in a Dominate mode.

Top management therefore has to have a keen understanding of who is who in the organization. This calls for a much tighter co-operation with the human resources function. The human resource managers must therefore also have a better overview of the strategic activities and *understand* the strategic direction! The CEO and upper echelon managers will ultimately be responsible for the "allocation" of the key strategic resource – the right people in the right places! Who is put in charge of what projects is crucial. Typically, there is a limited amount of talent available to run central, strategic projects, so it is important that key players are not spread too thin.

Above all, top management must be heavily involved in monitoring and reviewing the progress of each strategic program, including the human resource re-allocation that will be necessary following "reclassification" of strategic initiatives from pioneer to Rapid

Expansion (or, alternatively, abandon) and from Rapid Expansion to Dominate (or, alternatively, here again, abandon). As the project evolves, the most important role for top management, with support from the human resource function, is to ensure that new people are brought into the strategic initiative and second, that executives who were previously central to the project are re-assigned to other tasks.

The Strategic Entrepreneurs

In the past, we saw a strong, central role for division managers and business unit managers in the development of a company's various business strategies. Now, division managers can no longer be alone in this task. Of course, the typical Dominate/Defend strategies will continue to be seen as the role of the traditional division manager, strategic business unit manager, product manager and country manager. However, a number of additional managers will now have the chance to take strategic initiatives, particularly when it comes to Pioneering and/or Rapidly Expanding. These managers will thus now have legitimate roles as part of (or in charge of) particular strategic initiatives for pioneering/rapidly expanding. Strategic project management could, however, become a rare commodity given the various demands of being able to network, to work in a horizontal mode and to know where to find resources within the organization. Interpersonal relationship capabilities, with strong doses of cross-cultural sensitivities (given the frequently global nature of much pioneering/rapid expansion), will also be critical. The roles of these strategic entrepreneurs can thus be described as catalysts in project networks.

The Strategic Planner

Over the last decade, the strategic planner's function has gone through turbulent redefinition. The days of the large formal planning staffs and the corporate strategist's office are long gone. In some companies, the planning function has entirely disappeared. Today, however, the planner's role is perhaps more central than ever, but in a different way. Now, the planner is a catalyst for implementing entrepreneurial efforts for generating internal growth. The planner will have to work closely with the human resources function, to ensure that the most appropriate people are assigned to the various strategic tasks. One might even see the two functions becoming more and more blurred. Furthermore, the planner will have to play an important role in enhancing a consistent, tailored approach towards different types of strategic initiatives, depending on whether they are of the Pioneering, Rapid Expansion, or Dominate kinds. Here close co-operation with the controller function will be increasingly called for. Also, we may see an emerging trend towards a much closer integration between the planning, control and human resource management functions and processes.

Conclusions

This article argued for the need to shift the strategy formulation and implementation paradigms towards responding to greater pressure for enhanced internally-generated business growth. This challenge can only be met, in today's global, flatter organizations, by emphasizing human resources, the firm's competence base as the key strategic resource. Good strategies are thus the result of having the best people in the most appropriate assignments to support various strategic initiatives.

We have suggested a way for the members of an organization to identify new unique business opportunities in a more entrepreneurial mode and also emphasized the need to mobilize organizational capabilities to take advantage of strategic opportunities. A conceptual framework, with four strategic archetypes, emerged from this: Pioneer, Rapid Expansion, Dominate and Restructure. It was noted that, since the focus of this article is on growth, no further reference was made to the issues surrounding restructuring.

Five suggestions were made for strengthening the planning and control process to be more responsive to the unique needs for focus required for each strategic archetype. These guidelines for tailoring relate to how to identify and articulate the main tasks for each strategic context, how to compose an appropriate management team, how to enhance a unique dominant learning mode, how top management's mode of interaction might need to be tailored and, finally, how to instill a more flexible, multifaceted approach to strategic control.

It was then argued that perhaps the most demanding challenge is to manage the evolution of the various strategic initiatives as they develop from one archetype stage to another, calling for realignment of the strategic processes supporting them. Criteria for when and how to evolve from one stage to another were discussed.

Finally, the roles of the key players in the strategic process were discussed. The CEO and his top management group will have to place different emphasis on the various interfaces within the organization – catalyst vis-à-vis pioneer, analyst vis-à-vis rapid expansion cases and strategist vis-à-vis defense-type strategic settings. Line executives have a "mandate" to be more entrepreneurial with new business growth, complementing their classical strategic dominate roles. The planners' changing role is seen as perhaps the most dramatically changed one, now involving *both* an increased co-operation with the human resources management and control functions, *and* a primary responsibility for ensuring the dynamic, tailor-made management process support for each strategic initiative. Perhaps a fitting new label for the planner will be Chief Strategy Implementation Officer!

References

1. B. Chakravarthy and P. Lorange, *Managing the Strategy Process: A Framework for a Multibusiness Firm,* Prentice-Hall, Englewood Cliffs (1991).
2. B. Chakravarthy and P. Lorange, *op. cit.*
3. P. Lorange, Editor *Implementation of Strategic Planning,* Prentice-Hall, Englewood Cliffs (1982).
4. P. Lorange and R. F. Vancil, *Strategic Planning Systems,* Prentice-Hall, Englewood Cliffs (1977).
5. H. Mintzberg, *The Rise and Fall of Strategic Planning,* The Free Press, New York, NY (1994).
6. R. Amit and P. J. H. Schoemaker, Strategic Assets and Organizational Rent, *Strategic Management Journal* **14,** 33-46 (1993); J. B. Barney, Strategic Factor Markets: Expectations, Luck and Business Strategy, *Management Science* **32** (10), 1231-1241 (1986a); J. B. Barney, Firm Resources and Sustained Competitive Advantage, *Journal of Management,* **17,** 99-120 (1991); I. Dierickx and K. Cool, Asset Stock Accumulation and Sustainability of Competitive Advantage, *Management Science,* **35,** 1504-1511 (1989); R. P. Rumelt, Towards a strategic theory of the firm, In R. B. Lamb (ed.), *Competitive Strategic Management,* Englewood Cliffs, NJ: Prentice-Hall, pp. 556-570 (1984); B. Wernerfelt, A Resource-Based View of the Firm, *Strategic Management Journal,* **5,** 171-180 (1984).
7. T. E. Vollman, *Achieving Market Dominance Through Radical Change,* Harvard Business School.
8. T. E. Vollman, C. Cordón and J. Heikkilä, *Skanska & Rockwool: Making the Supply Chain Partnership Work,* case no. POM 184 (1996).
9. P. Brabeck-Letmathe, Growth and Operational Excellence are Keys to 1997, *Nestlé 2000* **4,** 1-3 (1997).
10. J. Meurling and R. Jeans, *The Ugly Duckling,* Ericsson Mobile Communications AB, Stockholm, Sweden (1997).
11. Sony Corporation, *Sony Design,* Tokyo, p. 7 (1997).

12. Global Strategy – GM Is Building Plants In Developing World To Woo New Markets, *Wall Street Journal Europe,* August 5, pp. 1 and 12 (1997).

13. B. Chakravarthy and P. Lorange, *op. cit.* See also P. Lorange, Strategic Planning for Rapid Profitable Growth, *Strategy and Leadership,* **24,** 42-48 (1996).

14. J. Piaget, *Le Structuralisme,* Presses Universitaires de France, Paris (1968).

15. H. J. Leavitt, Some effects of certain communication patterns on group performance, *Journal of Abnormal and Social Psychology* **46,** 38-50 (1951); H. J. Leavitt and L. T. Whisler, Management in the 1980's, *Harvard Business Review* **36** (6), 41-48 (1958).

16. R. Descartes, *A Discourse on Method,* Everyman, New York, NY (1994).

17. W. H. Newmann, *Managerial Control,* Science Research Associates, Chicago, IL (1984).

Strategic Control

Strategic Control for Fast-moving Markets: Updating the Strategy and Monitoring Performance

Raman Muralidharan

Raman Muralidharan is a Lecturer in Management at Indiana University, South Bend, IN, USA.

Source: *Long Range Planning*, Vol. 30, No. 1, pp. 64–73.

Authors often use the term 'strategic control' to describe a managerial process which is different from traditional management control. However a cursory look at the strategic control literature indicates that, while some of the managerial processes which are called strategic control are different from those associated with management control, others are similar. This led us to ask: is strategic control different from the traditional notions of management control? If so, in what way?

The objective of this article is to clarify the concept of strategic control by analysing differences between various approaches to strategic control and by examining whether, and in what way, strategic control is different from management control.

Koontz,[1] in an early effort at synthesizing the principles of management control, observed that: "In order to see the managerial function of control in proper perspective, it must be regarded in light of the other functions of the manager." In the same way strategic control should be understood within the context of well established concepts of planning and control, and in terms of its role in the overall management process. We will, therefore, briefly discuss the established concepts of planning and control and produce a model of the management process as described in management theory. We will then use this as a frame of reference to discuss the various strategic control approaches. Finally, we will compare the different approaches and identify the distinguishing aspects of strategic control.

Planning: Control and the Management Process

Definitions of planning and control include:

> "Planning – the selection from among alternatives of enterprise objectives, policies, procedures and programs. Control - the measurement and correction of activities of subordinates to make sure that plans are transformed into action."[1]

"Although planning and control are closely related, most managers see planning as the establishment of objectives or goals and the selection of rational means of reaching them, and regard control as the measurement of activities accompanied by action to correct deviations from planned events. It may thus be perceived that the function of managerial control is to make sure that plans succeed."[2]

"Control in organizations follows logically from the planning process. Its underlying rationale or purpose is to ensure that the organization is achieving what it intends to accomplish. Planning involves the setting of objectives or determination of some future desired state of affairs; the control process tracks performance against desired ends and provides the feedback necessary to gauge or evaluate results and take corrective action, as needed."[3]

Identical or similar descriptions of planning and control can be found throughout scholarly writings in management. A model of the management process which emerges from the above descriptions of planning and control is illustrated in Figure 1.

Strategies (or plans) are made during the planning stage of the management process. During strategy implementation control systems track actual performance, and the deviations from the planned performance levels are used to inform corrective action. The process of tracking actual performance and utilizing deviations to inform corrective action ensures that strategies are implemented as planned.

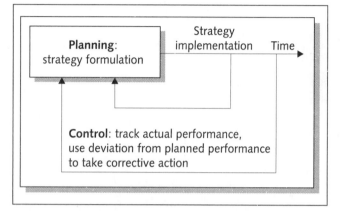

Figure 1. The management process.

Throughout this article we will refer to the established concept of control described above as 'traditional management control'. In addition we use the words 'plan' and 'strategy' interchangeably.

Various Approaches to Strategic Control

The Control of Strategy Implementation

In this approach strategic control is conceptualized as the managerial task which ensures that strategies are implemented as planned. For example, Schendel and Hofer[4] define strategic control in terms of its role in the overall strategic management process: "Strategic control focuses on the dual questions of whether: (1) the strategy is being implemented as planned; and (2) the results produced by the strategy are those intended." Harrison[5] characterizes strategic control as follows: "[S]trategic control is designed to permit management to ensure that actual outcomes are in conformity with the outcomes integral to the strategic choice." Bungay and Goold[6] observe that "A strategic control system ensures that the immense effort often put into preparing lengthy and detailed strategic plans is in fact translated into action."

The objective of this type of strategic control is identical to those of traditional management control. Its approach, however, is quite different. While the focus of traditional management control is on all aspects of the plan, the focus of strategic control is just on the key success factors.[6] To illustrate the difference in focus, Bungay and Goold[6] describe strategic controls in Honda:

> "[Honda] monitors customers satisfaction ratings very closely. Honda supplements industry surveys with the company's own research which focuses on ascertaining the cause of problems. An overriding goal of Honda's senior management is to come top of these ratings ... [Senior managers at Honda] pursue their second major goal in a more informal way ... This goal, which they take as seriously as the customer ratings, is to have high levels of 'employee excitement' in all departments. 'Employee excitement' is monitored by senior managers who are expected to visit their departments and report on it on a regular basis. In addition to these two strategic controls, a host of operational factors (such as utilization, machine break-down rates, cycle times, waste levels, etc.) are measured at each Honda plant ... but they have a different status from the two strategic controls, which are regarded as fundamental."

This process of strategic control starts with the identification of key success factors or those few elements critical to the success of the plan. Once these key success factors are identified, the rest of the steps in the strategic control process involve developing performance standards for the key success factors, measuring actual performance on these areas and utilizing the deviation to inform corrective action.[6,7] This process of exercising control, except for the identification of key success factors, is identical to the process of exercising traditional management control.

Validating Strategic Assumptions

This approach to strategic control assumes that the number of elements and their interactions in a firm's environment defy complete understanding; hence planning involves making assumptions about them. For this reason planning is inherently selective.[8] Consequently, the focus of management during strategy implementation cannot simply be to ensure that strategies are implemented as planned. Organizations should take plans as a starting point whose validity should be checked, and the question of whether the plan is still valid should be asked continuously.[8-10]

The process of validating strategic assumptions involves collecting and interpreting data, and generating appropriate responses. Data collection is performed at all levels of the organization since, as Schreyogg and Steinmann[8] observe, "different individuals have access to various data ... [therefore] a broad scattering of observational activities and a general attitude of strategic awareness is required". Interpretation of the data is by a group involving both line and top managers, and the decision to respond by changing the strategy rests with the top management.[8]

The purpose of strategic control in this approach is to control the strategy content itself as opposed to ensure the implementation of strategy as planned, and the managerial process is also different from the one associated with traditional management control.

This approach to strategic control, therefore, is fundamentally different from the traditional notion of management control.

Managing Strategic Issues

The approach to strategic control described above focused on the fact that the complexity of a corporation's environment at a given point in time (during planning) is difficult to understand without making simplifying assumptions, and hence the assumptions underlying the plan should be monitored continuously to check if the plan is still valid.

There is a related issue which is equally important. Even if the environment can be fully understood during the planning stage, the environment changes during the course of strategy implementation. These changes bring about new opportunities/threats which may render the existing plan obsolete. This problem arises because planning is periodic while the environmental changes are continuous. An approach to strategic control, which is also referred to as 'strategic issues management' (SIM) addresses this problem.[11,12]

SIM systems involve identifying significant changes in the environment and responding to them continuously during the course of strategy implementation.[11] The list of issues scanned is large enough to ensure that a wide variety of issue sources are covered. The task of scanning the environment and interpreting the data collected is performed by a specialized staff department in large organizations and by a group of "two to three top managers [who] put on staff hats" in small organizations.[11] Response to the data is based on the assessed impact of the issue and the urgency of the response required. If the response can be postponed, the issue is listed as an input for the next planning exercise. If the response required is urgent, it is made during strategy implementations usually in the form of adding a new project to the existing ones in the plan. The addition of new projects or deletion of certain elements in the plan as a response to the issues identified amounts to making changes to the content of the plan itself. The SIM approach to strategic control, therefore, is aimed at controlling the content of strategy as opposed to controlling the implementation of strategy. The managerial process involved is also different from that involved in exercising traditional management control.

Interactive Control

Another approach described as strategic control is Simons'[13] interactive control.[14] Simons argued that since traditional management control processes seeks to identify and correct deviation from plans, they are diagnostic tools and do not pay attention to the environmental changes which organizations encounter day after day. To be successful, however, organizations need to respond to opportunities and threats which emerge as a result of changes in the environment. Interactive controls help organizations meet this need.[13]

Simons defines interactive controls as "formal systems managers use to involve themselves regularly and personally in the decision activities of subordinates".[13] Interactive control is not a unique type of control system but is merely a diagnostic control system used interactively, consequently, a control system used interactively in one organization mar be used diagnostically in another.[13] Top managers choose any one aspect of the organization's performance and control it in an interactive fashion. Actual performance in this chosen area is monitored with respect to predetermined targets on a continuous basis. Detailed explanations are prepared by line managers for deviations from planned performance and the explanations are reviewed interactively by the top and line managers. The line managers, in the course of developing explanations, search and collect data on changes in the environment. The implications of the environmental changes are debated and discussed during the interactive review of the line managers' explanations for performance deviations. This process of monitoring actual performance, preparing explanations and discussing the explanations is performed frequently – as frequently as once a week in some cases. The review of explanations becomes a forum to debate and identify alternative ways of reaching objectives, in light of the environmental situation prevailing at the time of the review. For example, during John Scully's tenure at Pepsi, Neilsens ratings were used as an interactive control system. Pepsi's product market performance as reflected in Neilsens ratings was used as a forum to discuss, debate and identify tactical moves. [13]

Although the interactive controls are implemented by using a traditional control system interactively, the intent is not to ensure the implementation of strategy as planned but to generate strategic moves and new ways of doing things which reflect opportunities and threats faced by the organization at that point in time during implementation. Interactive control, thus, is aimed at controlling the content of strategy.

Periodic Reviews of Strategy

This approach to strategic control involves performing a full-scale review of the strategy periodically at pre-scheduled intervals. The objective of the review is to make necessary changes to the strategy if the assumptions made during the planning stage do not hold or if changes in the environment since the last periodic review present new opportunities or threats. The scope of the review, as the term full-scale indicates, is wide enough to cover all planning assumptions and all segments of the firm's environment. The frequency of such reviews, because of the wide scope of the process, is usually once in one or more years. [15] While some of the changes in the environment may be high profile and very noticeable like the oil crisis, many of the changes are low profile and, viewed in isolation, may represent a minor impact on a firm's strategy. Cumulatively these low profile changes, however, may represent a major impact on strategy. Newman[9] argues that periodic strategy reviews are an essential source of identifying and assessing the cumulative impact of such creeping changes which may otherwise go unnoticed. In organizations which perform periodic strategy reviews, line managers collect and report data on the validity of planning assumptions and environmental changes; interpretation of the data and response generation is performed through discussion and debate between line and top managers. [15]

Key Characteristics of Strategic Control

Table 1 summarizes the key characteristics of the five approaches to strategic control discussed above, along with those of traditional management control.

The purpose of strategic control in the first approach is the same as that of traditional management control. The managerial process suggested is also similar to those identified with traditional management control and involves setting standards, measuring actual performance and using deviations to advise corrective action. The only difference is that unlike traditional management control which focuses on the entire implementation process, strategic control focuses on the key success factors. The first approach to strategic control, thus, is only marginally different from the traditional notion of management control. The other four approaches to strategic control are, however, substantially different from traditional management control. The objective of strategic control in these four approaches is to control the content of the strategy, as opposed to ensure the implementation of the strategy as planned. The managerial processes used to effect strategic control in these approaches are also quite different from the process involved in exercising traditional management control.

By consolidating the four approaches aimed at controlling the content of strategy into one combined system, the five approaches to strategic control can be classified into two broad categories – one aimed at controlling the *implementation* of strategy and the other aimed at controlling the *content* of strategy. In what follows, we attempt to consolidate the four approaches aimed at controlling the content of strategy. Later, we will present a

	Traditional management control	Strategic control as the control of strategy implementation	Validating strategic assumptions	Strategic issues management	Interactive control	Periodic strategy review
Purpose	Ensure that strategy is implemented as planned	Ensure that strategy is implemented as planned	Change strategy content in light of invalid planning assumptions	Change strategy content in light of emerging opportunities/threats	Change strategy content in light of emerging opportunities/threats	Change strategy content in light of invalid planning assumptions and new opportunities/threats
Process	Set standards for performance, measure actual performance, use deviations to take correction action	Set standards for performance, measure actual performance, use deviations to take correction action	Collect data to monitor planning assumptions, interpret the data and respond to the information contained in the data	Collect data to identify opportunities and threats, interpret the data and respond to the information contained in the data	Choose an aspect of the organization's performance, track actual performance and debate the detailed explanations for deviations prepared by line managers	Collect data to check the validity of planning assumptions and to identify new opportunities/threats, interpret the data and respond to the information contained in the data
Focus	Implementation process in all its detail	Key success factors	Planning assumptions	Potential opportunities/threats which arise from the environment (including remote segments)	Environmental changes associated with the aspect of organizational performance chosen to be controlled interactively	Planning assumptions and potential opportunities/threats which arise from the environment (including remote segments)

Table 1. Management control and the five approaches to strategic control

comparison of the two broad approaches to strategic control with the traditional notion of management control and also illustrate the two broad approaches to strategic control using a case study. We then conclude the article with a discussion of managerial implications.

Combining the Four Approaches

All four approaches have their strengths and weaknesses, and a comprehensive strategic control system aimed at controlling the content of strategy should include the best elements of all four approaches. To develop such a comprehensive system, we compare the four approaches along the following dimensions: 1. trigger for changing the strategy content; 2. timing of the process; 3. nature of the decision process. The comparison along the three dimensions is summarized in Table 2 and is detailed below.

	Validating strategic assumptions	Strategic issues management	Interactive control	Periodic strategy review	A combined system
Trigger for changing the strategy content	Invalid planning assumption	New opportunity/ threat	Sizable deviation of actual performance from the plan	Invalid planning assumption or a new opportunity/ threat	Invalid planning assumption or a new opportunity/ threat
Timing	Continuous	Continuous	Continuous	Periodic	Continuous, including a periodic full-scale strategy review
The managers involved in the process	Line managers	Experts and staff	Line managers	Line managers	Line managers

Table 2. Developing a combined approach to strategic control aimed at controlling the strategy content

Trigger for Changing the Strategy Content

The trigger for changing the strategy content when validating strategic assumptions is the identification of an invalid planning assumption which may render the current strategy inappropriate. In the SIM approach the trigger is an indication that a new opportunity or threat has emerged. The trigger in the periodic strategy review approach is a combination of the two. In the interactive control approach the trigger is a sizable deviation from expected level of performance in the organizational area which is chosen to be controlled interactively. When deviations from planned performance levels are used as a trigger, there is no effort to change the strategy content if actual performance is in line with the plan. This is a problem, however, because although the actual performance may be in line with the plan, the plan itself may be incorrect, and hence a genuine need for changing the strategy content could be missed. The trigger for changing the strategy content when validating strategic assumptions and for the SIM approach, however, relies on data from the environment and is independent of the organization's performance with respect to the plan. These approaches, therefore, follow triggers which are more reliable indicators of the need to change the strategy content.

Timing of the process Strategic control in the periodic strategy review approach, as the label indicates, is performed periodically – usually once in one or more years. The strategic control process in the other three approaches, however, is active continuously during the course of strategy implementation. Relying on a periodic strategy review, performed once a year or less frequently, risks pursuing a strategy which is based on invalid assumptions for too long and not adapting to emerging opportunities and threats soon enough. It is, therefore, imperative for the strategic control process to be continuous to effect timely changes to strategy. The periodic strategy review, when used in conjunction with the continuous process, however, can serve the useful purpose of assessing the cumulative impact of environmental changes which have emerged since the last periodic strategy review.[9]

Nature of the decision process The nature of the decision process involved in making changes to strategy is important because, as Mintzberg[16] observes, if strategic decision processes are 'off-line', i.e. performed by staff experts who are removed from the day-to-day management activity, the exercise may become a sterile effort, and the environmental changes tracked as well as the decisions made will have very little relevance to what is really necessary.

Involving line managers in the process ensures that the information is interpreted from multiple perspectives and allows the line managers to bring their experience and creativity to bear on the issue. In addition, since the line managers are closely involved with the functioning of the organization, they are intimately aware of the emerging strengths, weaknesses and capabilities in their respective areas, and their involvement in the process ensures that decisions are made in light of the updated set of organizational capabilities, strengths and weaknesses. Ideally, therefore, the decision process should be 'on-line', involving line managers in the process as much as possible. Among the four approaches, the SIM approach emphasizes the use of experts and staff departments and hence advocates an 'off-line' process. The other three approaches, however, emphasize the involvement of the line managers individually or in groups and hence are more 'on-line'.

A system that combines the best aspects of the four approaches is one where the strategy control process is continuous and includes a periodic full-scale strategy review. The trigger for changing the strategy content, in such a combined approach, is the identification of an invalid planning assumption or a new opportunity/threat. In addition, the decision process in the combined approach is on-line, involving line managers to the extent possible in the tasks of data collection, interpretation and response generation.

Two Broad Approaches to Strategic Control

Table 3 presents the comparison of the two broad approaches to strategic control with traditional management control. As the table indicates, the response to our research question of whether, and in what way, strategic control is different from management control depends on which of the two broad approaches one adopts. Strategic control in the first approach is different only in terms of its focus on key success factors and only marginally different from traditional management control. If one adopts the second approach to strategic control, however, it is different in terms of the purpose, the managerial process and the focus. Strategic control in the second approach is, therefore, fundamentally different from the traditional notion of management control.

	Management control	Strategic control as the control of strategy implementation	Strategic control as the control of strategy content
Purpose	Ensure that strategy is implemented as planned	Ensure that strategy is implemented as planned	Change the strategy content in light of invalid planning assumptions and emerging opportunities/threats
Process	Set standards of desired performance, track actual performance and use deviations to take corrective action	Set standards of desired performance, track actual performance and use deviations to take corrective action	Collect data to monitor the validity of planning assumptions and to identify opportunities/threats, interpret the data and respond to the information contained in the data
Focus	All aspects of strategy implementation	Key success factors	Planning assumptions and potential opportunities/threats

*Table 3. Differences between
management control and strategic control*

The first approach is consistent with the model of the management process established in the management literature, to the extent that management is still seen as a negative feed-back activity where planning sets the direction for the organization, and control activities merely ensure that the organization implements the plans without deviation. The second approach, however, adds substantially to update this model. In the updated model of the management process (see Figure 2), strategies are formulated during the planning stage. The plans, however, are taken only as a start, and the strategy content is controlled during the course of its implementation by the second approach to strategic control. Management control, as in the established model, tracks actual performance with respect to all aspects of the plan and utilizes the deviations from the plan to inform corrective action. The first strategic control approach focuses on the actual performance of the organization with respect to key success factors and utilizes the deviations from planned performance to correct the implementation process. Taken together, the three control systems seek to ensure that the organization implements its chosen strategies and that the chosen strategies are appropriate.

A Case Study

The Saturn car project illustrates the use of the two broad approaches to strategic control. The post oil shock period of the 1970s and the early 1980s left General Motors, which was then principally a large car manufacturer, vulnerable to foreign competition which entered the US market offering small fuel-efficient cars. In an effort to reassert its competitive position in the automobile industry, GM launched the Saturn project in 1983.[17] The strategy for the Saturn project involved designing and building a new small car, which would compete head-on with the imported small cars while not taking away sales from GM's other car divisions.[17] The specific elements of this strategy

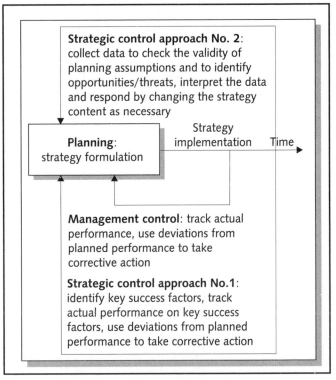

Figure 2. An updated model of the management process.

included the following: set up a separate car division – the sixth within GM – invest a total of 5 billion dollars in the project; build and operate a manufacturing capacity of 500,000 cars a year; utilize a revolutionary manufacturing process with heavy emphasis on automation; build a line of sub-compact cars with a gas consumption of 45-65 mpg; price the car at $6000.[17,18]

Roger Smith, GM's chairman at the time, and his management team identified key success factors for the project:

1. To lower manufacturing costs to match those of foreign automobile makers. In 1983 the per unit manufacturing cost of the foreign manufacturers was estimated to be $2000 lower than that of GM.[19]
2. The car ought to match or exceed the imported cars in quality and design.[18]
3. The customer service provided should far exceed existing levels to reclaim customer confidence and trust.[18]

Smith and his management team monitored the implementation progress with their attention on the key success factors (the first approach to strategic control). They also set up systems to ensure that implementation proceeded as planned with respect to all operational detail (the traditional management control). In addition, Smith and his management team actively procured, processed and responded to information on environmental changes and planning assumptions (the second approach to strategic control).

With time, during the implementation process, the concern for fuel-efficiency among automobile buyers had diminished as fuel prices stabilized. In addition, the foreign automobile makers moved away from subcompact size cars to relatively bigger compact size cars and sports coupes. With this shift, the foreign automobile makers effectively raised the small car buyers' expectations.[18] Smith and his management team recognized that these changes in the external environment rendered some elements of their initial strategy obsolete and modified their strategy. In addition to the changes in the external environment, changes within the organization also induced GM to modify its strategy for Saturn. Smith and his management team realised, from their experience with automation in other GM divisions, that their assumptions about the technical and economic feasibility of a highly automated manufacturing facility was not valid.[18] This recognition caused them to drop the original strategy of relying heavily on automation and to adopt a traditional mix of labour and automation instead.[18] In addition, the increase in global competition and the consequent deterioration in GM's financial position induced them to scale back investment plans from $5 billion to $3 billion.[18] Figure 3 summarizes the changes in GM's strategy for Saturn between 1983, when the project was planned, and 1990, when the first of the cars rolled out to the market.

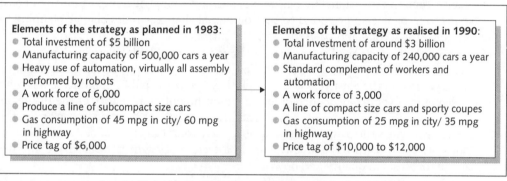

Source: Here comes GM's Saturn, *Business Week*, 9 April 1990

Figure 3. A summary of the changes to GM's strategy for Saturn between 1983 and 1990.

As this case illustrates, the recognition and response to environmental changes and invalid planning assumptions (the second approach to strategic control) resulted in changes to the content of GM's strategy for Saturn. These changes allowed GM to offer a car which matched the current customer expectations rather than those which existed during planning but had since changed. As a result, GM is well on its way to realizing the project's goal of developing a small car that would allow the company to regain its strong competitive position in the automobile market. By 1992, the car had won several awards for design, innovation and customer satisfaction. Sales had also exceeded targets. The project has been widely acclaimed a success.[20]

The exercise of the first approach to strategic control also had its unmistakable effects on the project's success. Smith's concern and commitment to bridge the $2000 cost gap resulted in several innovations in the areas of design, manufacturing and materials technology. These innovations, including the perfection of lost-foam casting, the development of a new automatic transmission system and the use of advanced plastics, have contributed significantly to lower the manufacturing costs.[18,21] The concern and commitment to match or exceed the imports in quality and design resulted in a revolutionary labour agreement which includes among other features a provision that ties product quality to worker pay.[20,22] It also motivated Smith and his management team to accept a delay in the roll-out of certain models when workers and engineers wanted to make minor but important modifications to the car's design just before the scheduled roll-out date.[23] These commitments have paid off in the form of design awards and customer satisfaction.[20] The commitment to exceed existing customer service levels resulted in the creation of a new dealer network for Saturn and the development of several service features intended to enhance the car buying experience.[20] It also resulted in a decision to promote the company (the Saturn division) and its image through repeated advertisements emphasizing the innovative spirit at Saturn and its dedication to quality and customer service. These efforts have created a strong brand loyalty for Saturn, in addition to strong sales.[20]

Managerial Implications

This analysis holds three important implications for managers:

1. Managers must be aware that strategies are always based on assumptions which need to be verified. Also environmental changes can make strategies obsolete. Therefore, in addition to utilizing control systems to monitor implementation (the first approach to strategic control and the traditional management control systems), it is important to establish systems to recognize and respond to environmental changes and to change planning assumptions (the second approach to strategic control).

2. Since even the best planned strategies may have to be modified during implementation, managers need to be prepared to retract their commitment to pre-planned courses of action. As we saw in the Saturn case, although they had made public commitments to certain elements of the strategy, including the establishment of a 'factory of the future' involving heavy use of automation, Smith and his management team drew back from this commitment when the planning assumptions were found to be invalid. As a result, GM avoided being left with huge investments in a technology which would have imposed unacceptable costs in quality and downtime.

3. The lack of staff support can hamper efforts to change pre-planned strategies even if top managers recognize the need to change the strategy and have the will to initiate the changes. Managers must build broad support for the changes by keeping staff informed of the developments that require changes in the strategy and by involving them in the decision-making process.

References

1. H. Koontz, Management control, a suggested formulation of principles, *California Management Review* **1**, 47-55 (1959).
2. H. Koontz and R.W. Bradspies, Managing through feedforward control, *Business Horizons,* June, 25-36 (1972).
3. L. G. Hrebiniak and W. F. Joyce, *Implementing Strategy,* Macmillan, New York (1984).
4. D. E. Schendel and C. W. Hofer, Introduction, In D. E. Schendel and C. W. Hofer (eds), *Strategic Management,* Little Brown, Boston, MA (1979).
5. F. Harrison, Strategic control at the CEO level, *Long Range Planning* **24** (6), 78-87 (1991).
6. S. Bungay and M. Goold, Creating a strategic control system, *Long Range Planning* **24** (3), 32-39 (1991).
7. C. H. Roush and B. C. Ball, Controlling the implementation of strategy, *Managerial Planning,* November/December, 3-12 (1980).
8. G. Schreyogg and H. Steinmann, Strategic control, a new perspective, *Academy of Management Review* **12**, 91-103 (1987).
9. W. H. Newman, *Constructive Control,* Prentice-Hall, Englewood Cliffs, NJ (1975).

10. J. F. Preble, Towards a comprehensive system of strategic control, *Journal of Management Studies* **29**, 391-409 (1992).

11. I. H. Ansoff, Strategic issues management, *Strategic Management Journal* **1**, 131-148 (1980).

12. P. Lorange, F. Scott Morton and S. Ghoshal, *Strategic Control Systems,* West Publishing Company, St Paul, MN (1986).

13. R. Simons, *Levers of Control: How Managers Use Innovative Control Systems to Drive Strategic Renewal,* Harvard Business School Press, Boston, MA (1995).

14. D. C. Band and G. Scanlan, Strategic control through core competencies, *Long Range Planning* **28** (2), 102-114 (1995).

15. M. Goold and. J.J. Quinn, *Strategic Control: Establishing Milestones for Long-term Performance,* Addison Wesley, Reading, MA (1993).

16. H. Mintzberg, *The Rise and Fall of Strategic Planning: Reconceiving Plans, and Planners,* The Free Press, New York (1994).

17. Chairman's letter to the Stockholders in the *10K Reports of General Motors* (1983).

18. J. B. Treece, Here comes GM's Saturn: more than a car, it is GM Corp. re-inventing itself, *Business Week* **9**, 56-62:1990).

19. D. Whiteside, R. Brandt, Z. Schiller and A. Gabor, How GM's Saturn could run rings around old-style carmakers, *Business Week* **28**, 126-127 (1985).

20. D. Woodruff, J. B. Treece, S. Wadekar and M. Lowry, Saturn: GM finally has a winner, but success is bringing a fresh batch of problems, *Business Week* **17**, 86-91 (1992).

21. S. A. Wood, GM unveils Saturn, lots of plastics, and new way of working with suppliers, *Modern Plastics* **67** (10), 16-18 (1990).

22. M. Edid, How power will be balanced on Saturn's shop floor, *Business Week* **5**, 65-66 (1985).

23. J. B. Treece, Are the planets lining up at last for Saturn?, *Business Week* **8**, 32-34 (1991).

The Balanced Scorecard: a Necessary Good or an Unnecessary Evil?

Stella Mooraj, Daniel Oyon, Didier Hostettler

Stella Mooraj is a Doctoral Candidate in the Department of Management Control at the Ecole des HEC, University of Lausanne. Her thesis compares the organisational motivations for the implementation of a Balanced Scorecard in multinational organisations with the actual benefits and disadvantages experienced. Her research interests include strategic control and performance measurement in an international environment.

Daniel Oyon is Professor of Management Control and Director of the Master of International Management Programme (MIM) at the Ecole des HEC at the University of Lausanne. His teaching and research interests centre on business strategy, management control systems, innovation and international business.

Didier Hostettler is Manager at Tetra Pak International, Lausanne, where for nine years he has worked in such fields as purchasing, control, and intelligent systems in Switzerland and the US. He took a key rôle in establishing the Balanced Scorecard at Tetra Pak Americas.

Source: *European Management Journal* Vol. 17, No. 5, 1999, pp. 481-491.

The Balanced Scorecard has emerged in recent years as what can perhaps best be described as a strategic control tool. Although surrounded by much publicity in bothprofessional and academic circles, few organisations are yet in a position to quantify its benefits, therefore investing time and money for unquantifiable results. The question posed in this article is whether or not the Balanced Scorecard is a necessary good, an unnecessary evil ... or perhaps, a necessary evil ... for such organisations.

Through a discussion of current literature on the topic and various examples, the article demonstrates that the Balanced Scorecard is a 'necessary good' for today's organisations. It is a tool which adds value by providing both relevant and balanced information in a concise way for managers, creating an environment which is conducive to learning organisations and eliminating the need for managers to 'choose' which type of control system to use at any given time. However, the article also draws attention to the fact that the entire Balanced Scorecard implementation process relies on both formal and informal processes, and that there are written and unwritten rules which must be considered for the process to be implemented successfully.

The Balanced Scorecard: a Necessary Good or an Unnecessary Evil?

The Balanced Scorecard has emerged in recent years as what can perhaps best be described as a strategic control tool. Its high-profile in management seminars and academic debates has placed the Balanced Scorecard alongside approaches such as Activity Based Costing/Management and Total Quality Management in terms of industry literary attention. The propaganda surrounding the Balanced Scorecard provides evidence that it is the key for driving performance in organisations; that it transforms strategic management paradigms by placing the emphasis on the enablers instead of on the results; and that it is the cockpit which provides all relevant strategic information. According to Kaplan and Norton (1996b), 'The Balanced Scorecard provides managers with the instrumentation they need to navigate to future competitive success'. They claim that it ' ... addresses a serious deficiency in traditional management systems: their inability to link a company's long-term strategy with its short-term actions'; Roger Bosworth, Senior Manager, Business planning and performance at NatWest UK says that 'Building the Scorecard is when you start to get your hands on those measures and drivers that are at the heart of a solid performance management system'. With statements such as these, it is no wonder that many organisations are falling over themselves to implement such a system. Using the Balanced Scorecard 'bible' (the original publication by Kaplan and Norton) as a reference, supported by internal or external consultants, organisations are changing their management system to conform with the Balanced Scorecard ethos.

Few organisations are yet, or will ever be, in a position to conduct a cost-benefit analysis for the Balanced Scorecard and therefore invest substantial amounts of time and money for unquantifiable results. In terms of the literature, the only scent of criticism comes from Atkinson *et al.* (1997) for whom the Balanced Scorecard does not cohere with their stakeholder approach to performance measurement. Perceiving the Balanced Scorecard as a performance measurement system, they argue that the key to such a system is that it 'focuses on one output of strategic planning: senior management's choice of the nature and scope of the contracts that it negotiates ... with its stakeholders' and that the 'performance measurement system is the tool the company uses to monitor those contractual relationships'. They criticise the Balanced Scorecard as failing to:

- highlight employee and supplier's contributions (that it doesn't consider the extended value chain, which is an essential element of today's networked organisations);
- identify the role of the community in defining the environment within which the company works;
- identify performance measurement as a two-way process (that is focuses primarily on top-down performance measurement).

If we accept the definition of the Balanced Scorecard as a strategic control system, then another of its key critics is Simons (1990) who condemns researchers who promote 'strategic control systems', arguing that they '... do not understand fully the means by which strategic control has been achieved.' He states that '...strategic control can be achieved by using familiar systems in special ways that recognize how strategies are formulated and implemented in organizations'. He continues ... 'In this sense, managers do use controls strategically, but without resorting to specialized strategic control techniques. The result of this process is an unobtrusive, yet effective, control of strategy.'

What then of the Balanced Scorecard? Is it a necessary good for today's organisations, an unnecessary evil ... or perhaps, a necessary evil ...? This article will attempt to answer these questions by investigating the role of the Balanced Scorecard within an organisation, including its fit with existing management control systems. The Balanced Scorecard will be deemed to be 'good' if it adds value to the organisation, and will be considered 'necessary' if it proves to be essential to management.

An introduction to the Balanced Scorecard

The Balanced Scorecard was first identified and implemented by Kaplan and Norton as a performance management tool, following a one-year multi-company study in 1990. Its aim is to present management with a concise summary of the key success factors of a business, and to facilitate the alignment of business operations with the overall strategy. It '… provides a medium to translate the vision into a clear set of objectives. These objectives are then further translated into a system of performance measurements that effectively communicate a powerful, forward-looking, strategic focus to the entire organization' (Kaplan and Norton, 1989).

1. Relevant and Balanced Information

One of the primary motivations in developing the Balanced Scorecard was that top management were being overwhelmed with data and were spending too much time analysing these rather than on making decisions. A further intention was to overcome the bias of existing management information towards financial measures. The Balanced Scorecard paradigm is that the financial results are obtained by successful implementation of strategic initiatives in the key business perspectives – as opposed to being their driving force.

2. Four Perspectives

The original Balanced Scorecard design identified four perspectives which are *the financial* perspective; *the customer* perspective; the *internal-business-process* perspective; and *the learning and growth* perspective. The perspectives represent three of the major stakeholders of the business (shareholders, customers and employees), thereby insuring that the holistic view of the organisation is used for strategic reflection and implementation. The importance with each of these perspectives (no matter how many are chosen to be necessary) is that the perspectives themselves and the measures chosen are consistent with the corporate strategy. Figure 1 shows how the Balanced Scorecard provides a framework, through these four perspectives, for translating strategy into operational themes and thereby facilitating the role of management.

The *financial perspective* represents the long-term objectives of the company. The measures chosen will represent the relevant stage in the product or service life-cycle and are summarised by Kaplan and Norton (1996a) as rapid growth, sustain and harvest. Financial objectives for the growth stage will be largely based on sales volumes, existing and new customer relationships and process development. The sustain stage on the other hand will be represented by measures analysing return on investment such as return on capital employed, discounted cash flow and perhaps economic value added. Finally, the harvest stage will be based on cash flow analysis with measures such as payback periods and revenue volume.

The *customer perspective* consists of measures relating to the most desired (i.e. the most profitable) customer groups. It will include several standard measures such as customer satisfaction and customer retention though in each case these should be tailored to meet the organisational requirements. Market share, customer value and customer profitability are other key measures that enable an organisation to create a clear vision of the customers whom it should target together with the identification of their needs and expectations from the company.

The *internal-business process perspective* focuses on the internal processes required in order for the company to excel at providing the value expected by the customers both productively and efficiently. These can include both short-term and long-term objectives as well as incorporating innovative process development in order to stimulate improvement. The internal-business perspective is particularly effective during a period of change as it focuses actively on the key processes required in order to implement the change programme efficiently.

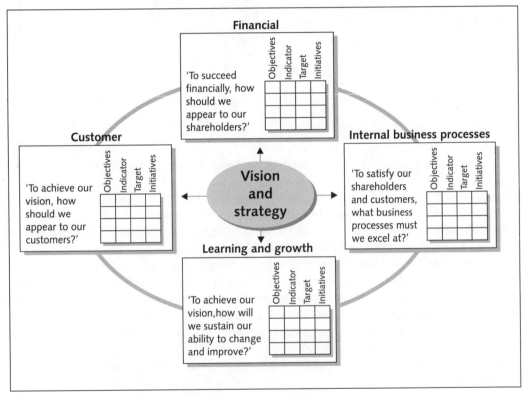

Figure 1. The balanced scorecard framework [Kaplan and Norton (1996a, p. 197)]

The *learning and growth perspective* focuses on internal skills and capabilities, in order to align them to the strategic goals of the organisation. The Balanced Scorecard process will often identify gaps between the required and existing skills and capabilities. Using it to identify strategic initiatives and related measures, these gaps can then be addressed and closed by initiatives such as staff training and development.

3. Cause-and-Effect Relationships

Identifiable cause-and-effect relationships are an important aspect of the Balanced Scorecard when choosing the appropriate indicators. It enables the translation of a financial aim, such as increasing revenue by x%, into operational factors which will lead to that increased revenue. Therefore, by evaluating the relevant factors in each segment of the Balanced Scorecard which may have an impact on a financial aim, the appropriate measures can be identified and the alignment of actions to the strategic goals is facilitated. Figure 2 demonstrates how the financial aim of increasing return on capital employed was translated at Tetra Pak into operational factors for each of the Balanced Scorecard segments. It clearly demonstrates the hypothesised cause-and-effect links which can be tested using the Balanced Scorecard measurement process. The diagram also shows the emphasis on growth as a means of obtaining the increased ROCE (Return On Capital Employed).

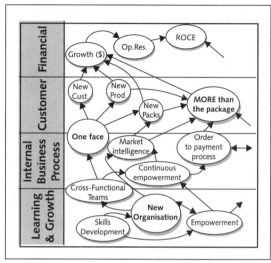

Figure 2. An example of cause-and-effect links within Tetra Pak

The Role of the Balanced Scorecard

Since its introduction as a performance measurement tool in 1991, an increasing number of roles have been identified for the Balanced Scorecard. These range from providing the critical information to be used in a strategic reflection process, to being a key part of the management system of the organisation whereby 360° feedback can be obtained on both the strategic objectives and the indicators being used to measure its attainment. This more comprehensive role can be seen in Figure 3 which demonstrates the role of the Balanced Scorecard as the 'king pin' of a management system.

Although the Balanced Scorecard will have a role to play in each of the four sections of the management system, often one or two of the sections will dominate. This will depend on the motivation for developing the Balanced Scorecard and on its stage of implementation. For example, in Europe, many organisations are implementing the Balanced Scorecard with an emphasis on planning rather than on control. They use the BSC as a tool for encouraging all managers to think strategically about the organisation and its future. As such, emphasis is placed on the strategic feedback and learning, and on the communications sections of the management system. Examples of companies which have developed one particular function of the Balanced Scorecard include Whirlpool, British Airways World Cargo and Tetra Pak. Whirlpool, the domestic appliance manufacturer, has implemented its Balanced Scorecard as a means of creating a performance culture within its European subsidiaries. British Airways World Cargo implemented their Balanced Business Scorecard as a means of accompanying and measuring the achievement of change and improvements during a major transformation process. As can be seen from the insert, Tetra Pak uses this new management system as a way of supporting strategic implementation in its local companies in order to gain enhanced feedback from all areas of the business.

Although a very similar Balanced Scorecard implementation process is pursued by many organisations, it produces different measures and different Balanced Scorecard roles according to the company dynamics and competitive position. This can be demonstrated by some of the case studies developed by Kaplan and Norton (Mobil USM&R, Cigna property and assurances and Skandia insurance), all of whom had the same external influences for implementation, yet all of whom convey different advantages of the Balanced Scorecard. For example, within Mobil, the ability to communicate the strategy to all members of the organisation and to obtain valuable feedback and ideas from employees nearest the customers was expressed as one of the key benefits obtained from the process. Within Cigna, a fundamental advantage came from the ability to link the Balanced Scorecard measures for each employee to an internal share price. This dramatically improved productivity as it meant that each individual reconsidered his/her role within the organisation, and concentrated on areas in which he/she could add value to the business. The motivation for this came from the fact that each employee owned internal shares and could win or lose according to overall company performances, as perceived internally. Finally, with the Skandia case study, we witnessed the first attempt at using the Balanced Scorecard as a tool for external communications. Although this was perhaps not the major advantage for Skandia, it demonstrates that the Balanced Scorecard has communication potential as a holistic system, which encompasses all stakeholders of the business.

The above discussion and examples tend to suggest that the Balanced Scorecard does indeed improve on current systems in a variety of ways. It provides relevant and balanced information in a concise way for managers, thereby reducing the time for 'digestion' of information and increasing the time for decision-making. It also creates an environment which is conducive to learning organisations through the testing of hypotheses regarding cause-and-effect relationships and by laying the groundwork for a 360° feedback process. Given the demands of today's competitive environment, these aspects enable us to conclude that the Balanced Scorecard is a 'good' system for management. However, many systems have been proposed in the past which aimed at adding value to management. Whilst some of them have been desirable to have, not all of them could be described as being 'necessary'. The question remains therefore, is the Balanced Scorecard 'necessary'?

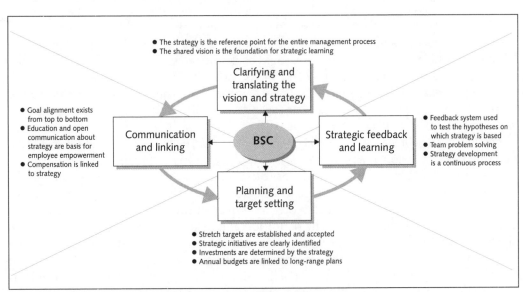

Figure 3. A management system for strategic implementation [Kaplan and Norton (1996a, p. 197)]

The Balanced Scorecard and Strategy

In Simons' criticism of strategic control systems, he relies on the definitions put forward by Schendel and Hofer (1979) who state that strategic control 'focuses on whether (1) the strategy is being implemented as planned, and (2) the results produced by the strategy are those intended' and by Lorange *et al.* (1986) who define a strategic control system as: '… a system to support managers in assessing the relevance of an organization's strategy to its progress in the accomplishment of its goals and, where discrepancies exist, to support areas needing attention.' As Simons points out, these definitions lead to a perception of strategic control systems as a process for keeping strategies on track and essentially parallel strategy formation with planning and strategy implementation with control. There is therefore a lack of the unplanned, no room for spontaneous reflection, and no place for the management of the unintended strategy (a function of culture, efforts to correct what was seen as misguided in the first place and miscommunications) which, according to Mintzberg, makes up a substantial part of the emergent strategy of an organisation.

Simons goes on to discuss the array of formal control systems available to management. He describes these as 'diagnostic control systems' (which periodically and systematically measure progress against plans, therefore concentrating on yesterday's strategies), 'interactive control systems' (which are those requiring regular management attention and discussion within the organisation, therefore focusing on the formation of tomorrow's strategies) and 'boundary control systems' (which are designed to communicate the boundaries of permissible activity to all employees in the organisation). Simons argues that top management will place the emphasis on the particular type of system that '… addresses the critical uncertainties that top managers perceive could threaten the achievement of their vision for the future', suggesting that only one of these systems will be the focus of management attention at any one time. He also stresses that the traditional view of planning and control and their relations with strategy formation and implementation should be inverted, as demonstrated in Figure 4.

Simons' discussion is essentially one arguing for the competencies of management to decide on which formal control system to place the emphasis on at any one time. However, there seems no logical reason why the managers should be forced to make this choice. It seems plausible that control systems could be developed which encompass diagnostic, interactive and boundary elements. After all, as perfectly demonstrated by Simons, each has its place within the organisation. In fact, if we bring the spotlight back on to the Balanced Scorecard, we can see that it does indeed combine elements of all three of the Simons' systems.

The Balanced Scorecard contains elements of a *boundary control system* in that it evolves from the vision, mission and strategic goals of the organisation. Its four perspective framework depicts limits in the organisation as it encourages employees to focus their attention on the key aspects of the business. If we refer back to the role of 'communication of strategy' inherent in many Balanced Scorecard implementation processes, we recognise it is a tool which could be used for the definition and dispersion of the core values of the organisation. Using the Balanced Scorecard in this way ensures that employees are aware of the mission of the organisation, of its major strategic goals and, more importantly, of the role that they have to play in their achievement. This perhaps facilitates the adherence to the core values outlined, as long as they are well understood by the employees. An example of the use of the Balanced Scorecard as such a system is demonstrated in the Tetra Pak example (see Figure 7).

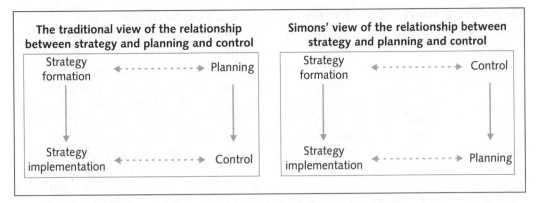

Figure 4. A comparison of the traditional view of the relationship between strategy and planning and control with that of Simons'

The Balanced Scorecard also contains elements of an *interactive control system* in that it reinforces the learning organisation theory by providing the possibility to test cause-and-effect relationship hypotheses, by forcing managers to look transversally at their organisation, and by providing a focus for 360° feedback. Depending on the competitive environment of the company, a strategic goal will be outlined and its achievement measured. This does not mean however, that all actions from then on in are passive, and consist purely of historical data. It is possible, or perhaps essential, to include proactive objectives on the Balanced Scorecard, which will advance the company towards its strategic goals and which, more often than not, will require a great deal of interaction. An example would be an organisation which wanted to be closer to its customer either in moving from a functional to process organisation or wanted to create cross-functional teams attached to specific customers. Without a great deal of interaction and top-management involvement, such an initiative would not be possible.

Finally, the Balanced Scorecard contains elements of a *diagnostic control system*. Its inclusion of lag indicators which measure the progress towards the achievement of objectives fits neatly into Simons' definition. However, as has been shown, these diagnostic measures are merely one part of a whole. This is demonstrated in the insert which explains how Tetra Pak benefits from the Balanced Scorecard as a boundary, interactive and diagnostic control system. The relationship between the three systems for a typical Balanced Scorecard is shown in Figure 5.

It seems plausible therefore that the Balanced Scorecard is a strategic control system which offers managers the possibility to combine all types of control systems and that, as such, it adds value to management. It allows the measurement of the performance of the current strategy, whilst enabling time and energy to be spent on the formation of tomorrow's strategies. This eliminates the need for managers to 'choose' which control system to use at any given time, thereby maximising the productivity of a holistic information base instead of using only partial information. It would therefore seem logical to argue that the Balanced Scorecard is a 'necessary' tool for today's managers. However, many seemingly 'necessary' and 'good' systems have fallen by the wayside due to their conflict with current systems. It is therefore important to spend a moment investigating the potential conflicts between the Balanced Scorecard and other existing systems.

The Balanced Scorecard and Existing Management Control Systems

Within an organisation, there exists a multitude of management control systems, both formal and informal. Every one of these systems influences behaviour, be it voluntarily or involuntarily. It is essential therefore that there is a coherence between the systems, and that employees receive a consistent message throughout the organisation and through time. The majority of traditional systems, such as planning and costing systems, aim at fulfilling one particular purpose – in this case resource planning and improved knowledge of costs. They appear to be standalone systems and, unfortunately, are often treated as such by management. In implementing such systems, management address one particular issue and are not always concerned with its cohesion with the strategic goals of the organisation. Effectively, they are healing a wound, without any conscious recognition of the importance of that wound when viewed as part of a whole. Perhaps more importantly, in many cases, it is their remuneration structure which encourages them to do so.

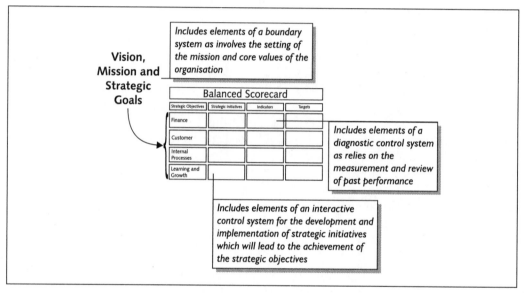

Figure 5. The balanced scorecard comprises boundary,
interactive and diagnostic elements of control

For example, a production manager who is remunerated for the profits of his unit may implement Activity Based Costing as a means to obtain more pertinent cost information with a view to reducing costs. On the other hand, the headquarters have identified a shortage of resources and wish all energy to be spent on the development of new products. It seems logical that whilst the manager is being remunerated according to his financial performance, he will forgo the requirements of headquarters and will continue to improve his own situation. By identifying a balanced set of financial and non-financial measures which are linked to the strategic goals of the organisation, it is possible to prevent such conflicts and to ensure that managers are being encouraged to conduct business in a manner which is rewarding to both him/herself and the organisation. Also, the implicit contract which is established in the identification of goals and performance measures ensures that goal congruence is achieved which in itself facilitates the task of management control systems.

Not only does the Balanced Scorecard provide a measurement framework which improves alignments of actions to the strategic goals of an organisation, but it also provides a platform for identifying priorities. During the identification of strategic initiatives which need to be implemented in order to achieve the various objectives, managers often find themselves inundated with ideas. By continually referring to the strategic goals which have been outlined, they are able to set priorities and to oversee the implementation of other projects, such as Activity Based Costing. This means that they have the complete picture and are able to identify the importance of each initiative with this in mind.

Although the Balanced Scorecard is designed to become a key part of the management system of an organisation, it is rarely introduced as such from the beginning. Although many managers will state from the outset that the Balanced Scorecard will become the king-pin for all strategic and performance measurement systems, they will often run it parallel with current systems at least in the beginning in order to insure themselves against initial teething problems. Also, achieving a complete Balanced Scorecard is a time-consuming process and often the benefits of implementing an incomplete pilot outweigh the advantages of waiting for the completion of the Balanced Scorecard before introducing it within the organisation.

The adoption of the Balanced Scorecard will have a direct impact on the other management control systems of the organisation and vice versa. In order to gain the necessary buy-in from employees, it is important to demonstrate that the Balanced Scorecard method is not merely a supplement to current systems which simply adds work, and not value, to the organisation. Therefore, it is essential to identify the advantages of the Balanced Scorecard from the beginning, to communicate them to the organisation and, more importantly, to ensure that they are achieved. For example, it is not sufficient to state that the Balanced Scorecard will replace current monthly reports if, for an indefinite period, the two reports are produced together.

Often, the Balanced Scorecard will require the collection of new data which, in turn, will require new collection systems and often new responsibilities. As has been proved time and time again within organisations, there is a tendency to resist change. Therefore, in order to ensure a smooth transition to the Balanced Scorecard process, a communications exercise is essential in order to explain the process, to clarify rumours, and to use the informal systems to the advantage of the process as opposed to its disadvantage. This exercise will need to be tailored to the organisation, which means that it should be tailored to the various cultures that it hosts.

The Balanced Scorecard and Culture

The Balanced Scorecard will be affected by three major types of culture – national culture, occupational culture and, perhaps most importantly, the culture of the organisation. *National culture* affects the Balanced Scorecard primarily in terms of the approach towards financial performance. For example, organisations in the United States consider it to be their duty, and their overriding goal, to maximise shareholder wealth (i.e. to optimise the return on investment ratio). On the other hand, European organisations have long been concerned with a stakeholder approach whereby all those with an input in the organisation are rewarded. These different cultural paradigms will have an influence not only on the development of the Balanced Scorecard, but also on its acceptance. It is certainly apparent that many European organisations are hesitant about it as they consider that they have been using balanced perspectives for years. Indeed, in France, the *tableau de bord* is a relatively old management control system which provides a mass of quantitative information. It could be argued therefore that the Balanced Scorecard adds different value in each of these cases. For the US organisations, it forces them to look beyond the short term financial results to the strategic health of the organisations. For the Europeans, on the other hand, it helps them to reduce the wealth of indicators currently 'produced' in order to obtain a more pertinent selection of strategically important indicators.

National culture is also of relevance when it comes to defining performance indicators within international organisations. A prime example can be found in the customer perspective of the Balanced Scorecard and in the commonly used 'customer satisfaction index' indicator. It seems evident that a customer satisfaction index in Japan (where satisfaction is based largely on intangibles, such as long-term relationships) should be constructed differently to one in the United States (where satisfaction relies on tangible aspects such as reducing lead time). Such aspects would therefore have an impact on the creation of the Balanced Scorecard for an international organisation.

In terms of *occupational culture*, the Balanced Scorecard will be affected by traditions. It has been noted by many researchers in the field of organisational behaviour that certain occupations have their own defined culture which consists largely of unstated, informal rules. A Balanced Scorecard which attempts to use formal indicators to change behaviour and go against these traditions is likely to be unsuccessful and therefore such cultures must be considered when designing the Balanced Scorecard.

Finally, *organisational culture* has the potential to have a large impact on the Balanced Scorecard, be it positive or negative. It is generally considered that national and occupational cultures override an organisational culture, as is implied by Pugh (1993) when he says that 'On organizational grounds, resistance to change can be understood when it is realized that, from a behavioural point of view organisations are coalitions of interest groups in tension'. However, Collins and Porras (1994), in their book entitled *'Built to Last'* imply that a strong organisational culture can in fact override any national or occupational differences, enveloping its employees in a 'cult-like' environment. Indeed, they pay homage to some of the world's most successful companies who have developed 'cult' cultures, by devoting an entire chapter to them.

The organisational structure put in place to implement the strategy also affects the role of the Balanced Scorecard. A decentralised organisation which relies on trust and autonomous decision-making for its success would employ the Balanced Scorecard in an entirely different way than a centralised organisation which relies on a top-down process of instructions and implementation throughout its hierarchy. Implementing the Balanced Scorecard which contradicts the management ethos of the organisation would create confusion throughout and would put in jeopardy the other formal and informal systems. The implementation of the Balanced Scorecard should therefore correspond not only to the formal strategic approach of the organisation, but also to the various informal cultures to which it is host.

The Balanced Scorecard and the Missing Elements

Recognition of the informal elements of management control systems is important if a new system is to be successful. Chapello (1996) demonstrates the extent of the informal systems in place through her identification of six major axes to be considered for management control. The elements which are highlighted in Figure 6 are those which are predominantly informal and over which the managers have little control ... perhaps giving justification to Dermer and Lucas (1996) who in 1986 wrote an article entitled 'The illusion of managerial control'. In their article, they suggest that a large part of the results of an organisation are due to elements outside of management control.

However, it is important to add that what cannot be measured is still relevant. It is essential to build into a Balanced Scorecard the potential for highlighting unforeseen events which may have changed the competitive environment of a company. Changes occur and must be taken on board if an organisation is to remain alert and proactive.

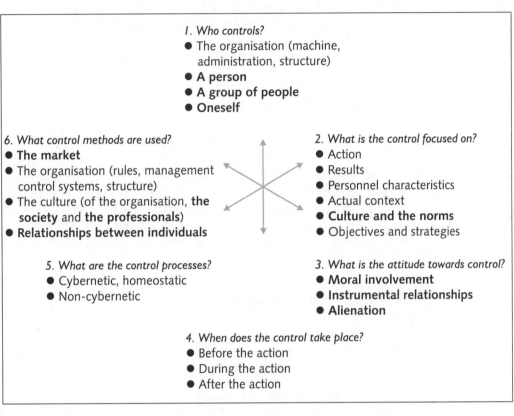

Figure 6. The six dimensions of analysis of means of organisational control

Conclusion

The above discussion demonstrates that the Balanced Scorecard is a 'necessary good' for today's organisations. It adds value by providing both relevant and balanced information in a concise way for managers. It creates an environment which is conducive to learning organisations within which hypotheses regarding cause-and-effect relationships can be tested and the groundwork for a 360° feedback process is laid. It also eliminates the need for managers to 'choose' which control system to use at any given time by incorporating aspects of boundary, interactive and diagnostic control systems. This enables management to maximise the use of a concise, holistic information base.

However, the entire Balanced Scorecard implementation process relies on both formal and informal processes, whether this be in relation to the strategic approach of the organisation and its corresponding structure, to the cultural aspects of the organisation, or indeed to the management control systems currently in place. In all of these areas, there are written and unwritten rules and these must be considered in order for any new process to be implemented successfully. Given that each organisation has its own combination of formal and informal, it is not surprising that each has a unique Balanced Scorecard and a unique priority for its implementation.

The key issue still to be addressed by research in the field of the Balanced Scorecard is that of cost-benefit. It would be of interest, both to companies who have made the move to the Balanced Scorecard and to those who are considering it, to know exactly how much value is added. However, given that many of the advantages are of an intangible nature it would be difficult to quantify them in a robust manner and to obtain satisfactory scientific evidence of the true value of the Balanced Scorecard. Perhaps managers will have to be content with case studies and articles which attempt to outline some of the advantages and disadvantages.

A balanced scorecard at Tetra Pak

Tetra Pak develops, manufactures and markets systems for the processing, packaging and distribution of liquid food. Tetra Pak produces packaging material at 57 plants and has 72 marketing offices around the world. Every day more that 200 million Tetra Pak packages are distributed in over 160 countries. Tetra Pak sales amounted, in 1998, to 11 billion CHF and 18, 200 people were employed (more on www.tetrapak.com). Tetra Pak contributes – together with its customers and suppliers – to the safe, efficient and environmentally sound production and distribution of liquid foods to the consumers of the world.

Tetra Pak Core Values

- Freedom with accountability
- Partnership with customers, suppliers and colleagues
- Long-term perspective
- Innovation and creativity
- Commitment & fun

Over the last 10 years, Tetra Pak has delivered a profitable financial performance as a result of its ambitious and forceful expansion in all possible countries. Nevertheless, the Group Management was still not satisfied with certain other aspects of the business. In practice, Tetra Pak management always relied on a very complete financial reporting package with very few non-financial figures notably in the organisational and external aspects. In fact, Tetra Pak has always been, and will most probably remain, a very 'decentralised' company giving a large range of autonomy to an array of small to large companies led by a robust local management. The glue that ties each operation to each other is a set of Corporate Core Values lead by a remarkable 'Freedom with Accountability' value. By spreading out such Corporate Core Values, Tetra Pak is bringing together some of the characteristics of a boundary control system which should lead to specific, key behaviours. On the other hand, establishing the yearly detailed Budget and following-up against actual performance throughout the year is the main control system that has accompanied Tetra Pak over the years. If this is combined with a few thought-provoking company presentations, the description of a typical diagnostic control system becomes apparent at Tetra Pak.

By launching a Balanced Scorecard initiative, the intent was to provide the market operations with a different way of thinking in order to follow more thoroughly the implementation of their generally well elaborated strategy. However, the Balanced Scorecard is not only about bringing a new reporting system. The reasoning behind it is that anticipating the critical success factors of such a strategy and their critical measurements is key to defining the unique path to short and long term prosperity in each market operation and service company. In fact, acting in mature markets such as Western Europe or North America or, on the contrary, in developing markets in Asia or Eastern Europe, where the way of doing business is different, stresses the importance of the distinct strategy and set of measurements in each area. For instance, in North America, the key success factors would relate more to the highly competitive price environment associated with high expectation on customer satisfaction. In China, critical success factors would be related to managing the high growth rate of the market and getting the organisation to perform adequately under increasing demand. Another important element of this initiative is the trend to link the employee's individual objectives and incentives to a Balanced Scorecard.

An additional advantage of deploying Balanced Scorecards is the alignment of measurements that help nurture knowledge sharing between operations and define the base for benchmarking from a continuous improvement standpoint. For instance, measuring customer satisfaction in a comparable manner should lead to superior and homogeneous products and services to Tetra Pak world-wide customers.

Also, sharing the Balanced Scorecard results and not the reporting formality, which is only directed as a control mechanism for management, helps employees to understand the priorities and objectives of their particular operations. Therefore, it was of the utmost importance to develop a comprehensive follow-up information system easily accessible by many, in this specific case, using a web-based application deployed in the Tetra Pak Intranet.

Moreover, a Balanced Scorecard will not, on its own, bring about improvements in long-term competitiveness and profitability. In fact, it is setting ambitious long-term targets – or stretch targets – accompanied by a comprehensive list of initiatives for each measure, which have proven to be the key drivers to better overall performance. Also 'setting the mind' of the employees to longer-term objectives will prop up the Balanced Scorecard as an instrument to help foster change. Ultimately, a Balanced Scorecard implementation should provide managers with useful information to allow a better decision-making process. (Figure 7) summarises the dynamic of the Balanced Scorecard at Tetra Pak and its function as a decision-making enabler. Note the feedback and learning phase that closes the loop and the close integration with the Budget exercise as resources are needed to perform the list of initiatives. In practice, if resources cannot be allocated it could be that the entire strategy or targets must be revisited. In conclusion, a Balanced Scorecard should be well integrated in the decision-making process of a company but not be additional indicators of the daily operational work. Its integration within the reporting system is seen as important but should not be the objective. In reality, a Balanced Scorecard will help the management to better communicate the strategy, to benchmark with other operations, to prioritise and to motivate the teams to common and longer-term goals. These last elements would therefore justify the investment of time in deploying and perfecting the Balanced Scorecard. Strong leadership and management skills are also essential for coping with the natural resistance that one would expect to find in any change agenda.

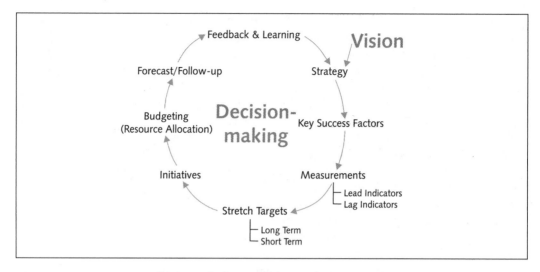

Figure 7. Balanced Scorecard at Tetra Pak

References

1. Atkinson, A.A., Waterhouse, J.H. and Well, R.B. (1997) A stakeholder approach to strategic performance measurement. *Sloan Management Review* **Spring**, 25-37.
2. Chapello, E. (1996) Les typologies des modes de contrôle et leurs facteurs de contingence: un essai d'organization de la littérature. *Comptabilité – Contrôle – Audit, Tome* 2, Vol. 2.
3. Collins, J.C. and Porras, J. 1. (1994) *Built to Last – Successful Habits of Visionary Companies.* Harper Business, New York.
4. Dermer, J. and Lucas, R. (1996) The illusion of managerial control. *Accounting Organizations and Society* **11**(6), 471-482.
5. Kaplan, R.S. and Norton, D.P. (1996a) *The Balanced Scorecard – Translating Strategy into Action.* Harvard Business School Press, Boston, MA.
6. Kaplan, R.S. and Norton, D.P. (1996b) Linking the balanced scorecard to strategy. *California Management Review* **39**(1).
7. Lorange, P., Scott Morton, M. and Ghoshal, S. (1986) *Strategic Control,* p. 10. West Publishing Company, St Paul.
8. Pugh, D. (1993) Understanding and managing organizational change. In *Managing Change,* eds C. Mabey and B. Mayon-White 2nd ed., pp. 108-112. The Open University.
9. Schendel, D. and Hofer, C. (1979) *Strategic Management: A New View of Business Policy and Planning,* p. 18. Little, Brown and Company, Boston.
10. Simons, R. (1990) Rethinking the role of systems in controlling strategy. Harvard Business School, note 9-191-091.